The Figs Table

MORE THAN
100 RECIPES FOR
PIZZAS, PASTAS,
SALADS, AND DESSERTS

Todd English
and Sally Sampson

Photographs by Carl Tremblay

SIMON & SCHUSTER

SIMON & SCHUSTER

Rockefeller Center

1230 Avenue of the Americas

New York, NY 10020

SIMON & SCHUSTER and colophon are registered trademarks

of Simon & Schuster Inc.

Book design by Deborah Kerner

Manufactured in the United States of America

1   3   5   7   9   10   8   6   4   2

Library of Congress Cataloging-in-Publication Data

English, Todd.

The Figs table : more than 100 recipes for pizzas, pastas, salads,

and desserts / Todd English and Sally Sampson ; photography by Carl Tremblay.

p.   cm.

Includes bibliographical references and index.

1. Cookery, Italian.   2. Cookery, American.   3. Figs (Restaurant).

I. Sampson, Sally, date.   II. Title.

TX723.E54   1998

641.5945—dc21   98-28035

CIP

ISBN 978-1-5011-9070-4

For OLIVER, ISABELLE,
and SIMON ENGLISH,
and LAUREN
and BENJAMIN SAMPSON,
our five little pizza eaters.
Extra cheese.
No green stuff.

Acknowledgments

We couldn't possibly thank or praise
Brad Stevens and Heather McDonald enough.
Without them we could never, ever,
ever have done this book.

The Figs Table

Todd's Philosophy of Pizza

SALLY: Why pizza?

TODD: I love food that you can eat with your hands. And I'm fascinated with pizza.

SALLY: Even so, there must have been *some* thing or *some* moment that got you going?

TODD: Many moons ago, when I was in my teens, I used to go to Pepe's Pizzeria in New Haven as often as possible. Their white clam pizza is the pinnacle for me of a certain style of pizza.

SALLY: What style is that?

TODD: A slightly thicker crust than Figs', but also light. Pepe's inspired me to do pizza.

What confirmed my decision was a pizzeria (though I can't remember the name) on a hilltop in Emilia Romagna. I was with a group of Italian friends, and we sat outside under a canopy surrounded by beautiful gardens. Outside the tent was a massive stone oven. We started with antipasto and went on to a selection of pastas, served family style, and then pizzas that never seemed to stop flowing. Pizza with zucchini flowers. Pizza with wild boar. Pizza with prosciutto and pizza with mussels. It made me feel that having a pizzeria was something I *had* to do someday.

SALLY: At Figs (and at Olives), you combine and layer ingredients that I would never have considered eating, so that when I eat at Figs I'm eating things I would never ordinarily eat. In fact, I'm eating things I don't even ordinarily like.

TODD: I hope so. That's part of the trust.

SALLY: What inspires your combinations?

TODD: Number one, I never forget that food is supposed to taste good. Number two, the classics inspire me. I simply rearrange them: I do not attempt to reinvent the wheel. And three, I add a pinch of craziness.

SALLY: One of the things that make a Figs pizza so unusual is that your crust is very thin, and the toppings are very sparse.

TODD: We have three sayings at Figs: "Never too thin and never too rich," "Less is more," and "Never trust a round pizza."

SALLY: Regarding "Never too thin and never too rich," isn't it a contradiction to say of sparse toppings "never too rich"?

TODD: No. I don't mean rich as in abundant. I mean rich as in depth of flavor. Remember: "Less is more."

SALLY: "Never trust a round pizza"?

TODD: If the dough is made right, the pizza will never be perfectly round. Our dough should be very wet and free-form: I might go so far as to say that the dough has a mind of its own. The dough determines what you do, not the other way around.

SALLY: Why don't you throw your pizza up in the air? Or why does anyone do it?

TODD: Our dough is different from dough that gets thrown up in the air. People who throw it use a tougher dough that gets stretched by centrifugal force, whereas we stretch our dough with a rolling pin. Figs dough is more delicate. I like to be able to eat more than one slice of pizza without feeling like a doughball myself.

SALLY: Is there a place for a thick crust?

TODD: Absolutely. But it should still be light. Just double the amount of Figs dough and roll it out to the same size that we suggest.

SALLY: Let's face it, not everyone is going to make pizza dough. How do you feel about people using premade dough?

TODD: It's okay. I've got to be realistic.

SALLY: What's more important, the crust or the topping?

TODD: You really need wheels to enjoy your car.

SALLY: When I was growing up, pizza meant tomatoes and cheese. What happened? Are your pizzas more authentic, or are they "designer" pizzas?

TODD: Figs pizzas are the result of what I experienced in Italy. I have eaten every pizza that anyone I know has considered a renowned or amazing pizza, and this is what has filtered out. I certainly don't have a problem with a pizza with tomatoes and cheese. In fact, I love it.

SALLY: What's your favorite Figs pizza?

TODD: The Classico. Tomato and shaved Parmesan. A small amount of Parmesan rather than a lot of mozzarella.

SALLY: Your least favorite?

TODD: I don't have one. It's like asking which is your least favorite child. I love them all. My children and my pizzas.

SALLY: What's your favorite nonpizza Figs meal?

TODD: Risotto.

SALLY: What are your favorite non-Figs pizzerias?

TODD: Pepe's in New Haven, da Buffeti in Rome, da Michele's in Naples, and al Forno's grilled pizza in Providence.

SALLY: Have you ever come up with a pizza that you thought was great, but no one ordered it?

TODD: Foie gras pizza. Foie gras and pizza are two completely different cultures, so it is a little bit of a stretch. Although I did think it was really good.

SALLY: What do you hate to see in a pizza?

TODD: Pizza should never be limp. It should be crispy on the bottom.

SALLY: What's the worse thing you've ever seen served on top of a pizza?

TODD: Ravioli pizza. Fried wonton pizza.

SALLY: What do you consider must-have pizza equipment?

TODD: A strong mind and a strong will. You have to be hardheaded and brave. Your tendency will always be to put more on top than you should. You must be able to hold back with toppings but not with the olive oil.

SALLY: Equipment?

TODD: An unglazed stone and a wooden peel, and that's it.

SALLY: What do you like to eat with pizza?

TODD: Salad.

SALLY: What's the best dessert to eat following pizza?

TODD: The Fig and Prosciutto pizza.

SALLY: Is that a serious answer?

TODD: Yeah.

SALLY: Best drink?

TODD: Beer.

SALLY: If not beer, what kind of wine? What about kids?

TODD: If not beer, red wine. Chianti. San Giovese. For kids, definitely Coke. This isn't an endorsement but—either that or a tall glass of birch beer.

SALLY: Why do you write cookbooks?

TODD: Because cookbooks are modern grandmas that teach us old and new ways of cooking. I actually learn things in the process. Just the fact that I can now write a recipe seems amazing. It seems that any time you try to teach something you learn more in the process.

SALLY: Why doesn't the food taste as good when I follow one of your recipes as it does when you make it?

TODD: Why is it that a carpenter can build something far better than I could ever conceive of building that thing myself, even with the right tools and the right design? Practice makes perfect. And as Rick Pitino (the coach of the Celtics) says, "Perfect practice makes perfect."

SALLY: What would you eat if stranded on a desert island?

TODD: It always comes back to pasta e fagioli.

SALLY: What do your kids like to eat?

TODD: McDonald's. We do occasionally stray to sushi—thankfully.

SALLY: What do you like to cook with your kids at home?

TODD: I don't spend a lot of time cooking with my kids, but I do like to bring them to the restaurant to be involved there.

SALLY: You said that you like to eat with your hands. What other than pizza?

TODD: Sandwiches. Sushi. Salads.

SALLY: I'm afraid to ask, but what's the largest number of pizzas you've eaten in a day?

TODD: I went on a pizza tour and went to 15 different pizzerias, so that's at least 15 different pizzas. There were other people, though.

SALLY: If you could share a pizza with anyone, who would it be?

TODD: My great-great-grandmother Bettina because I think she'd get a kick out of it and out of seeing what I've become. She didn't have much joy in her life, and I think I could bring a smile to her face.

Or Sophia Loren.

SALLY: Who do you try to please when you cook?

TODD: My wife.

SALLY: What's next?

TODD: Soups.

SALLY: What does that mean?

TODD: You'll see.

The Figs Pantry

Dry Goods

anchovy fillets, canned in oil and salt
artichoke hearts and bottoms, canned
baking chocolate (*Callebaut or El Rey*)
baking powder
baking soda
balsamic vinegar
black turtle beans
brown sugar, dark and light
canola oil
chickpeas, canned
chocolate, semisweet
chocolate, unsweetened
chocolate, white
cocoa powder (*Droste or Callebaut*)
confectioners' sugar
cornmeal, stone-ground yellow
cornstarch
flour, all-purpose
honey
mustard, Dijon grainy and smooth
oats, rolled

olive oil, virgin and extra-virgin

pasta, assorted shapes

rice, superfino arborio

salt, kosher

semolina

sesame tahini, canned

tomatoes, canned whole and
canned crushed

tomato paste

vegetable oil

white cannellini beans, dried
or canned

white sugar

wine, red and white

Dried Spices

Spices are best purchased in their most whole, natural state rather than pre-ground. At Figs, we like to grind our own spices in a coffee grinder, which results in a spice with more perfume. If you cook a lot, you'll find that it's worth having one grinder designated specifically for this use.

bay leaves

cardamom pods

cayenne

cinnamon, ground

cinnamon sticks

cumin seed, whole or ground

fennel seeds, whole

ginger, ground

nutmeg, whole or ground

paprika, Hungarian

peppercorns, black
red pepper flakes, crushed
saffron threads
vanilla beans, Tahitian
vanilla extract

Fruits and Vegetables

carrots
celery
garlic
gingerroot
lemons
limes
potatoes, Idaho and new
shallots
sweet potatoes
tomatoes, beefsteak or plum

Refrigerator

butter, unsalted
olives, assorted
Parmesan cheese, in a chunk
Romano cheese, in a chunk

Freezer

bacon, slab
butter, unsalted

The Figs Kitchen

Having good equipment won't make you a good cook, but it will make your life easier. Here's a list of what I like to have on hand.

blender

cheese grater

coffee grinder (*for grinding spices, especially peppercorns*)

colander

cutting board (*a big, heavy wooden one that won't move around*)

food processor

Japanese mandoline—A MANDOLINE IS A GRATER-LIKE DEVICE WHERE THE FOOD MOVES OVER A KNIFE BLADE TO ACHIEVE A CONSISTENT SHAPE. THERE ARE FRENCH, GERMAN, AND SWISS MANDOLINES, BUT I LIKE THE JAPANESE-MADE ONE BEST BECAUSE IT DOES A GREAT JOB, IS INEXPENSIVE, AND IS READILY AVAILABLE IN ASIAN MARKETS.

pizza cutter

pizza peel

pizza stone

ladles
measuring cups
measuring spoons
mixing bowls, stainless steel
mortar and pestle
sieve
slotted spoons
spatulas
tongs
vegetable peeler
whisks
wooden spoons

Pots and Pans

8-quart stockpot
8-inch cast-iron skillet
10-inch skillet
14-inch skillet
sauté pan

Knives

8-inch chef's
9- or 10-inch slicing
boning
paring
serrated bread

BASICS

Roasted Garlic

Always buy the freshest garlic you can find; the fresher it is, the sweeter it will be. The best garlic has firm, tissuelike skin and should not be bruised, sprouted, soft, or shriveled. If you find cloves that have tiny green shoots, be sure to discard the shoots; they will only add bitterness.

MAKES 2 GARLIC BULBS

2 garlic bulbs, unpeeled, tops sliced off
2 tablespoons olive oil
½ teaspoon kosher salt
¼ teaspoon black pepper

Preheat the oven to 400 degrees.

Place the garlic in a small baking dish and sprinkle with the oil, salt, and pepper.

Bake, uncovered, until the garlic is lightly browned and soft, about 25 minutes.

Use immediately, or cover and refrigerate up to 3 days.

Roasted Red Onions

Roasted red onions impart substantial richness and depth of flavor to many dishes, from classic roast chicken sauce to soup to pizzas to panini. They have a wholly different, mellow flavor, especially compared with raw or roasted white onions.

At both Olives and Figs, we roast 25 pounds of red onions at a time.

MAKES ABOUT 1½ TO 2 CUPS

3 pounds red onions, peeled and cut into ½-inch dice (about 4 to 5
*   onions)*
3 tablespoons vegetable or canola oil
1 tablespoon kosher salt
1 tablespoon plus ½ teaspoon black pepper

Preheat the oven to 350 degrees.

Place all the ingredients on a baking sheet and toss to combine. Transfer to the oven and roast until translucent, about 40 minutes, stirring occasionally to prevent blackening.

Use immediately, or cover and refrigerate up to 3 days.

Balsamic Onions

*T*he sweetness of roasted red onions is further enhanced by the combination of balsamic vinegar and sugar. I particularly like this Asian-influenced sweet and sour *agro dolce.*

We use these as a condiment on steak and burgers or placed on top of goat or Gorgonzola cheese on toast.

MAKES ABOUT 1½ TO 2 CUPS

3½ cups balsamic vinegar
½ cup sugar
3 pounds Roasted Red Onions (page 29)

Place the vinegar and sugar in a medium-sized saucepan and cook over medium-high heat until reduced by half, about 20 minutes. Add the Roasted Red Onions and cook until syrupy, about 10 minutes.

Use immediately, or cover and refrigerate up to 1 week.

Caramelized Onions

I am deeply, madly in love with onions. Caramelizing them adds another dimension of richness that further enhances their many uses. Caramelized onions can be used as a stuffing for ravioli, swirled into risotto, or simply used as a condiment to accompany almost any roasted meat or vegetable.

You can substitute leeks for a somewhat different but equally delicious flavor.

MAKES ABOUT 1½ TO 2 CUPS

1½ tablespoons unsalted butter
¼ cup vegetable or canola oil
3 pounds Spanish onions, peeled and thinly sliced

Place a large skillet over medium heat and when it is hot, add the butter and oil. Add the onions and stir. It is important to let the onions sweat before the sugar starts to caramelize. Cook until perfectly browned (not light but not too dark), about 40 minutes.

Use immediately, or cover and refrigerate up to 2 days.

Roasted Tomatoes

*T*his is a great way to concentrate the flavors of the tomato, and if you want to blister the skin, broil for 3 minutes at the end.

MAKES 12 TOMATOES

12 plum tomatoes
1 tablespoon olive oil
1 teaspoon kosher salt
½ teaspoon black pepper

Preheat the oven to 250 degrees.

Place the tomatoes on a baking sheet and rub with the oil. Sprinkle with the salt and pepper.

Roast until the tomatoes are shriveled and slightly darkened, about 3 hours.

Use immediately, or cover and refrigerate up to 4 days.

Three Flavored Oils

Although three different oils follow this note, I'm not a huge fan of flavored oils. However, when applied in the right way, using them almost as an essence, they give an extra layer of flavor to a dish. Never use them instead of olive or canola oil for cooking.

Basil Oil

We use Basil Oil primarily for Pizza Classico (page 157) or drizzled as a garnish on soups, polenta, risotto, and salads, where we use it instead of a basil leaf garnish.

MAKES ABOUT 1½ CUPS

1 small garlic clove, minced
1 cup fresh basil leaves
¾ cup vegetable oil
¼ cup olive oil
½ teaspoon kosher salt
¼ teaspoon black pepper

Place the garlic and basil in a food processor fitted with a steel blade and pulse until chopped. Add the oils, salt, and pepper and process until smooth.

Use immediately, or cover and refrigerate up to 5 days.

Mint Oil

We love this drizzled on Baba Ghanoush (page 72).

MAKES ABOUT ⅔ TO ¾ CUP

3 to 4 tablespoons fresh Italian flat-leaf parsley
Generous ½ cup fresh mint leaves
⅓ cup vegetable oil
2 tablespoons olive oil
¼ teaspoon kosher salt
Pinch black pepper

Place the parsley and mint in a food processor fitted with a steel blade and pulse until chopped. Add the oils, salt, and pepper and process until smooth.

Use immediately, or cover and refrigerate up to one week.

Chive Oil

Swirl this into Chive Risotto (page 141).
You can use scallion greens for a more intense flavor.

MAKES ABOUT ⅔ TO ¾ CUP

1 small garlic clove, minced
½ cup fresh chives
⅓ cup vegetable oil
2 tablespoons olive oil
¼ teaspoon kosher salt
Pinch black pepper

Place the garlic and chives in a food processor fitted with a steel blade and pulse until chopped. Add the oils, salt, and pepper and process until smooth.

Use immediately, or cover and refrigerate up to 5 days.

Fig Jam

ig Jam is more like a dried fruit preserve than a true jam. We use it primarily on our Fig and Prosciutto Pizza (page 162), but after you've tried it, I'm sure you'll come up with your own uses.

MAKES ABOUT 1 CUP

1 teaspoon canola or vegetable oil
3 shallots, diced
1 cup red wine
¼ cup Chicken Broth (page 40) or canned low-sodium chicken broth
¼ cup veal or beef broth
¾ cup balsamic vinegar
1 teaspoon chopped fresh rosemary leaves
¼ cup sugar
1 rounded cup dried mission figs, quartered

Place a medium-sized skillet over medium heat and, when it is hot, add the oil. Add the shallots and cook until they are softened, about 3 minutes. Deglaze with the red wine and reduce by half. Add the broths and vinegar, and reduce by half. Add the rosemary and sugar.

Lower the heat to low and cook until the sugar has melted, about 3 to 5 minutes. Add the figs and cook, stirring occasionally, until they are rehydrated, about 10 to 12 minutes. Cook until the mixture has the consistency of a liquidy jam, about 10 to 12 minutes.

Use immediately, or cover and refrigerate up to 5 days.

Focaccia

*F*ocaccia is a simple leavened flatbread. Serve it as an accompaniment to a meal, the base of a sandwich, or as a snack, warm from the oven.

MAKES 4 FOCACCIA

For the dough:

¼ cup whole-wheat flour

3½ cups all-purpose flour, plus additional for sprinkling

2 teaspoons (¼ ounce) fresh yeast

2 teaspoons kosher salt

2 teaspoons sugar

2 teaspoons extra-virgin olive oil

1⅔ cups lukewarm water

1 to 2 tablespoons stone-ground yellow cornmeal, for sprinkling

For the topping:

1 tablespoon extra-virgin olive oil

½ teaspoon kosher salt

¼ cup freshly grated Parmesan cheese

Place the flours, yeast, salt, and sugar in a mixer fitted with a dough hook. While the mixer is running, gradually add the oil and water. Knead on low speed until the dough is firm and smooth, about 10 minutes.

Divide the dough into four balls, about 7½ ounces each. Line two cookie sheets with parchment paper. Place two balls on a sheet and cover with a damp towel and let rise in a warm spot until doubled in bulk, about 1 to 2 hours, depending on how warm your kitchen is. (If it is warm, it will take less time.)

To prepare each focaccia: Place a ball of dough on a lightly floured surface and punch down with your fingertips until the surface is well dimpled.

One hour prior to cooking, place a baking stone or baking sheet in the oven and preheat it to 400 degrees.

Drizzle the surface of the dough with the oil and evenly distribute the salt and Parmesan cheese. Sprinkle the bottom with the cornmeal, place the focaccia in the oven, and bake until it is golden brown, about 15 to 20 minutes.

Serve immediately.

Chicken Broth

*I*ndispensable in my kitchen, but any good-quality, low-salt canned broth is an acceptable substitute.

MAKES ABOUT 12 TO 14 CUPS

6- to 7-pound chicken, trimmed of fat
Carcass, back, and neck from another 6- to 7-pound chicken
1 ham hock or bone (optional)
2 celery stalks, chopped
2 carrots, peeled, if desired, and chopped
1 Spanish onion, chopped
2 leeks, chopped
2 garlic cloves
2 bay leaves
1 bunch fresh thyme
1 small bunch fresh oregano
1 teaspoon whole black peppercorns
1 teaspoon kosher salt, or more to taste
½ teaspoon black pepper, or more to taste

Place the chicken, chicken parts, ham hock, celery, carrots, onion, leeks, garlic, bay leaves, thyme, oregano, and peppercorns in an 8-quart stockpot and cover with cold water.

Bring to a boil over high heat. Lower the heat to low, partially cover, and cook for 3 hours.

Strain and discard the solids. Add the salt and pepper. Cover and refrigerate. When cooled, skim off and discard the hardened fat.

Use immediately, or refrigerate up to 3 days.

STARTERS

Fennel, Watermelon, and Black Olive Salad with Feta Cheese

When I talked to Sally about this salad, she looked at me cross-eyed, which did not stop her from eating a hefty portion when I'd finished preparing it. I agree it's hard to imagine wrapping your taste buds around it, but if you think about it, it's simply a variation of *agro dolce*, the combination of salty and sweet. The classic pairing is prosciutto and fruit. I replaced the traditional honeydew with watermelon, which is too rarely paired with anything, and the prosciutto with the equally salty feta cheese. The fennel, a delightful cross between celery and licorice, adds texture and crunch. It is at its strongest when raw, which is just how I like it. It should be sliced as thin as possible. We use a Japanese mandoline (page 25), but a sharp knife will do.

Although it's not particularly Italian, this salad reminds me of sitting on a balcony in Tuscany, looking out at the walled city of Lucca. It is a perfect and refreshing picnic salad.

SERVES 6 TO 8 AS A STARTER

1 fennel bulb, thinly sliced (about 4 cups)
4 cups watermelon, seeded and cut in very large julienne
½ to 1 cup coarsely chopped black olives
1 red onion, thinly sliced (about 2 cups)
1 bunch scallions, greens only, chopped
¼ cup chopped fresh basil leaves
¼ cup fresh lemon juice
½ cup extra-virgin olive oil
2 tablespoons balsamic vinegar
1½ to 2 cups crumbled Bulgarian feta cheese (see note)
1 teaspoon kosher salt
½ teaspoon black pepper
4 ounces paper-thin prosciutto (optional), for garnish

Place the fennel, watermelon, olives, onion, scallions, and basil in a large serving bowl. Add the lemon juice, oil, vinegar, feta cheese, salt, and pepper and toss well.

Divide among 6 to 8 salad plates and serve immediately, garnished, if desired, with the prosciutto.

N O T E : We like Bulgarian feta for its full flavor, creamy texture, and crisp bite. If you can't find it, simply substitute French or Greek.

Roasted Carrot and
Feta Salad with *Za'atar*

I first tried this style of salad on mezza tables in Israel, and now I can't get enough. You can also substitute almost any root vegetable alone or in combination, including potatoes, parsnips, sweet potatoes, or beets.

You can certainly make this without the *za'atar*, but if you try it, you'll be glad you did. Although *za'atar* means "thyme" in Arabic, when used as a seasoning it usually refers to a mixture of sumac, dried thyme, marjoram, salt, and varying amounts of sesame seeds: The end result is a bit sour and tangy. Brad Stevens, Figs executive chef, prefers Jordanian *za'atar* for its lavish use of sesame seeds, but I prefer the Lebanese. *Za'atar* can be found in Middle Eastern and specialty food stores, or may be ordered from Penzey's, 1-414-574-0277.

SERVES 4 TO 6

2½ pounds carrots, peeled, if desired, quartered lengthwise and cut into
*   angled 1–inch slices*
2 tablespoons olive oil
¼ teaspoon kosher salt
¼ teaspoon black pepper
¾ cup crumbled Bulgarian feta cheese (see note on page 43)
2 tablespoons extra–virgin olive oil
1 tablespoon za'atar, *or more to taste*
¼ cup chopped fresh parsley or cilantro leaves

Preheat the oven to 425 degrees.

To roast the carrots: Place the carrots, olive oil, salt, and pepper on a baking sheet; toss well and transfer to the oven. Roast, shaking occasionally, until they are just beginning to brown, about 30 minutes. The carrots should be firm and not mushy. Transfer to a medium-sized serving bowl. Add the remaining ingredients and toss well.

Serve immediately, or cover and refrigerate up to 4 hours.

Overcooked, Overroasted Green Bean Salad

This salad was created out of my belief that the nouvelle cuisine rage of under-cooking vegetables was a farce. When you blanch a vegetable to get a bright *al dente*, you cook out all the nutrients; in this dish, you cook them all in. It sure isn't as pretty as a plate of bright green green beans, but it tastes great.

It is very important to mix all the ingredients together while they are still warm so that the flavors penetrate.

SERVES 4

1 pound green beans, trimmed
2 tablespoons olive oil
¼ teaspoon kosher salt
¼ teaspoon black pepper
½ cup diced slab bacon
1 red onion, thinly sliced
3 garlic cloves, minced
3 anchovy fillets, minced
1½ tablespoons balsamic vinegar
¾ to 1 cup coarsely chopped fresh basil leaves
½ teaspoon kosher salt
¼ teaspoon black pepper

Preheat the oven to 425 degrees.

To roast the green beans: Place the beans, oil, salt, and pepper on a baking sheet; toss well and transfer to the oven. Roast, shaking occasionally, until they are just beginning to brown, about 30 minutes.

While the beans are cooking, prepare the rest of the salad: Place a large skillet over medium-high heat and when it is hot, add the bacon. When the fat begins to render, add the onion, garlic, and anchovy fillets, stirring well after each addition, and cook until all are slightly caramelized, about 3 to 5 minutes. Pour off and discard the excess fat.

Off heat, add the vinegar and pour the mixture over the warm beans. Add the basil, salt, and pepper and toss well.

Transfer to a medium-sized serving bowl and serve immediately or at room temperature.

August Beefsteak Tomato Greek Salad

One of my favorite salads is the traditional Greek salad. At Figs, we rev up this variation with aromatic cilantro and pungent watercress and serve it on top of crostini brushed with Basil Oil (page 33).

We make so much of this salad that the tomato shark has become one of our favorite gadgets. A tool with a red handle and a small scoop at the end, it is perfect for effortlessly removing tomato cores.

SERVES 6

5 vine-ripe or beefsteak tomatoes, cored, halved, and sliced
*1 English cucumber or 2 slicing cucumbers, peeled, seeded, and sliced on
    a diagonal*
1 red onion, thinly sliced
1 teaspoon dried Greek oregano
½ cup roughly chopped fresh cilantro leaves
2 tablespoons extra-virgin olive oil
1 tablespoon fresh lemon juice
¼ to ½ teaspoon kosher salt
¼ teaspoon black pepper
1 bunch watercress, well washed and torn apart
3 ounces Bulgarian feta cheese, shaved (see note on page 62), for garnish

Place the tomatoes, cucumbers, onion, oregano, and cilantro in a large serving bowl and toss. Add the oil, lemon juice, salt, and pepper, and toss well.

Place the watercress on top and serve immediately, garnished with the shaved feta cheese.

Fava Beans with Orange Segments and Toasted Walnuts

If I were to die and be reincarnated a vegetable, I would like to be a fava bean, hiding inside that little stem, living inside a velvet room.

SERVES 4 TO 6

½ teaspoon kosher salt
2½ pounds fava beans, shelled
2 small oranges, segmented
½ red onion, diced
¼ cup chopped scallion greens

For the dressing:

1 tablespoon olive oil
¼ cup chopped walnuts
1 teaspoon minced fresh gingerroot
1½ teaspoons chopped fresh rosemary leaves
¼ cup fresh orange juice (about 1 orange)
½ teaspoon kosher salt
¼ teaspoon black pepper

Fill a large bowl with ice water.

Bring a large pot of water to a boil over high heat. Add the salt and beans and let return to a boil. Cook until the beans are bright green and tender, about 2 to 3 minutes. Drain, place in the ice water, and drain again.

Peel and discard the inner skin from the beans, and place the beans in a large serving bowl. Add the orange segments, onion, and scallion greens.

To make the dressing: Place a large nonreactive stainless steel, nonstick, or lined copper skillet over medium-high heat and, when it is hot, add the oil. Add the walnuts and cook until they are lightly browned, about 3 minutes.

Off heat, add the gingerroot, rosemary, orange juice, salt, and pepper, stirring well after each addition.

Pour over the fava beans. Cover and refrigerate at least 1 hour.

Cucumber Salad

*P*roving the adage "cool as a cucumber," this liquidy salad is great on Black Bean Chili (page 98) or Chickpea Burger (page 190) or drizzled on fresh tomatoes or on a ham or turkey sandwich.

SERVES 3 TO 4

1 cup plain yogurt (goat's milk, if you can find it)
1 English cucumber or 2 slicing cucumbers, peeled and sliced into thin
  rounds
½ medium-sized red onion, thinly sliced
1 teaspoon chopped fresh mint leaves, plus additional for garnish
½ teaspoon kosher salt
¼ teaspoon black pepper

Place the yogurt in a cheesecloth suspended over a small mixing bowl. Cover and refrigerate overnight.

Discard the liquid from the bowl and place the drained yogurt in a medium-sized serving bowl. Add the remaining ingredients. Cover and refrigerate at least 2 hours or up to 4.

Serve garnished with the additional mint leaves.

Fried Artichokes
with Anchovy Butter

*T*his is a dish that shows off Mediterranean cooking at its finest. For artichoke lovers, the combination of the fried artichokes, lemon, anchovies, and Parmesan cheese is what Mediterranean flavor is all about.

SERVES 4

4 small artichokes, stems and tough outer leaves removed
2 lemons, quartered
½ cup all-purpose flour
½ teaspoon kosher salt
¼ teaspoon black pepper
1 large egg, beaten
½ cup bread crumbs
¼ cup olive oil
2 tablespoons unsalted butter
1 anchovy fillet, minced
Pinch kosher salt
Pinch black pepper
4 to 6 cups mixed greens, well washed and chilled
Shaved Parmesan cheese, for garnish

Fill a large bowl with ice water.

Place the artichokes and 4 of the lemon quarters in a large nonreactive stainless steel, nonstick, or lined copper pot; cover with cold water; and bring to a boil over high heat. Lower the heat to medium and cook until the artichokes are tender, about 25 minutes.

Transfer to the ice water. Drain and remove the leaves and the fuzzy chokes. Trim off the edges of the bottoms and quarter them.

Place the flour, salt, and pepper on a large plate. Place the eggs in a shallow bowl and the bread crumbs on another large plate.

Dredge the artichoke quarters in the flour mixture and then in the eggs and then in the bread crumbs.

Place a large nonstick skillet over medium-high heat and when it is hot, add the oil. Add the artichoke quarters and cook until crispy and golden brown, about 1½ to 2 minutes on each side. Be careful not to overcrowd the skillet. Place the artichoke quarters on paper towels and drain well.

Reheat the skillet over medium heat and add the butter. Add the anchovies, salt, and pepper and cook until the anchovies are browned, about 1 minute. Add the breaded artichokes to the anchovy butter and stir until well coated.

Divide the greens between 4 salad plates and top each with equal amounts of hot artichokes.

Serve immediately, garnished with the remaining lemon wedges and shaved Parmesan cheese.

Roasted Beets with Walnut Gorgonzola Dressing

*U*nfortunately, beets are not on the top-ten list of favorite foods for many people. Most people hate them because they've only eaten them boiled or canned, but I was fortunate enough to try the real thing at an early age. So they're on *my* top-ten list, and this recipe might just be a great way to get them on yours. The roasting brings out the sweetness and intensifies the depth of flavor that is lost when you boil. Once you roast a beet, you'll never go back.

Don't throw away the beet greens: braise or sauté them if they are large, or add them to salad greens if they are small.

The rich, thick Walnut Gorgonzola Dressing is also great on burgers or grilled portobello mushrooms or mixed into greens.

SERVES 4 TO 6

1½ to 1¾ pounds beets, trimmed and halved
2 tablespoons olive oil
½ teaspoon kosher salt
¼ teaspoon black pepper
1 bunch arugula, well washed and torn apart

For the Walnut Gorgonzola Dressing:

2 tablespoons extra-virgin olive oil
¼ cup chopped walnuts
¼ red onion, thinly sliced
2 tablespoons chopped fresh basil leaves
1 tablespoon balsamic vinegar
¼ teaspoon kosher salt
3 ounces Gorgonzola cheese
¼ cup light or heavy cream

Preheat the oven to 425 degrees.

To roast the beets: Place the beets, 1 tablespoon olive oil, ¼ teaspoon salt, and ⅛ teaspoon pepper in a roasting pan and cook until the beets are tender, about 40 minutes. When they are cool enough to handle, remove the skins and slice the beets.

Place the beets in a medium-sized mixing bowl and toss with the remaining 1 tablespoon olive oil, ¼ teaspoon salt, and ⅛ teaspoon pepper.

To make the Walnut Gorgonzola Dressing: Place a large skillet over medium-high heat and, when it is hot, add the extra-virgin olive oil. Add the walnuts and cook until they are browned, about 2 to 3 minutes. Transfer to a small mixing bowl and when the walnuts have cooled to room temperature, add the onion, basil, vinegar, and salt.

Place the Gorgonzola cheese and cream in a blender or food processor fitted with a steel blade and process until smooth. Transfer to the bowl with the walnuts and mix to combine.

Divide the arugula between 4 to 6 plates and top with equal amounts of beets. Serve immediately with a large dollop of Walnut Gorgonzola Dressing.

Haricots Verts Salad with Mustard Vinaigrette

A classic.

SERVES 4 TO 6

1 pound haricots verts or green beans, trimmed
1 small red onion, thinly sliced
2 tablespoons extra-virgin olive oil
2 tablespoons fresh lemon juice
2 teaspoons Dijon mustard
1 teaspoon kosher salt
½ teaspoon black pepper

Fill a large bowl with ice water. Bring a medium-sized pot, filled halfway with water, to a boil over high heat. Add the beans and cook for 2 minutes. Drain, place in the ice water, and drain again. Place the beans and onion in a medium-sized serving bowl.

To make the dressing: Place the oil, lemon juice, mustard, salt, and pepper in a small mixing bowl and whisk until well combined. Pour over the beans and toss well.

Serve immediately.

Golden Beet and Prosciutto Salad

*M*y love for beets extends beyond the common red. If you can find white or candy-striped beets, try them in this recipe. The combination of sweet and salty is great, and the mint adds freshness.

SERVES 4

For the dressing:

1 heaping tablespoon Dijon mustard
3 tablespoons extra-virgin olive oil
3 tablespoons fresh orange juice
1 teaspoon balsamic vinegar
½ teaspoon kosher salt
¼ teaspoon black pepper

6 golden beets, roasted (see page 56) and sliced
2 tablespoons freshly grated Parmesan cheese
4 ounces thinly sliced prosciutto, torn into shreds
6 scallion greens, minced
7 mint leaves, chopped, for garnish

To make the dressing: Place the mustard, oil, orange juice, vinegar, salt, and pepper in a large mixing bowl and mix to combine.

Add the beets and toss well. Add the Parmesan cheese, prosciutto, and scallion greens and mix to combine.

Divide between 4 salad plates and serve immediately, garnished with the mint leaves.

Roasted, Fried Pear Quarters with Frisée, Prosciutto, and Balsamic Glaze

Frying and roasting in one dish may seem like a lot of work, but it's well worth it. Inspired by the classic combination of prosciutto and melon, I've substituted pears for the melon. The addition of the thick, almost chocolatelike balsamic glaze melds the two flavors together to create a heavenly dish.

SERVES 6

3 Bosc or Bartlett pears, unpeeled and quartered
4 tablespoons olive oil
1 teaspoon kosher salt
½ teaspoon black pepper
½ cup all-purpose flour
1 large egg, beaten
½ cup bread crumbs
2 cups balsamic vinegar
1 tablespoon sugar
5 ounces thinly sliced prosciutto
6 cups frisée
1 tablespoon fresh lemon juice
2 teaspoons extra-virgin olive oil

To roast the pears: Place the pears, 1 tablespoon olive oil, ¼ teaspoon salt, and ⅛ teaspoon pepper on a baking sheet and cook until the pears are tender but not limp, about 10 to 15 minutes. Set aside to cool.

To fry the pears: Place the flour, ¼ teaspoon salt, and ⅛ teaspoon pepper on a large plate. Place the eggs in a shallow bowl and the bread crumbs on another large plate.

Dredge the pear in the flour mixture, then in the egg, and then in the bread crumbs.

Place a large nonstick skillet over medium-high heat and when it is hot, add the remaining 3 tablespoons of oil. Add the pears and cook until crispy and golden brown, about 1½ to 2 minutes per side. Place on paper towels and drain well.

To make the balsamic glaze: Place the vinegar and sugar in a small saucepan and cook over medium heat until it has reduced to a syrupy, chocolate saucelike consistency and it drags on a spoon, about 20 minutes. It should be reduced to about 3 to 4 tablespoons.

Place about 4 to 5 prosciutto slices on each of 6 salad plates. The plate does not need to be completely covered. Top with frisée and drizzle with the lemon juice, extra-virgin olive oil, the remaining ½ teaspoon salt, and the remaining ¼ teaspoon pepper. Top with the fried pears and drizzle with the balsamic glaze. Serve immediately.

Insalata Bistecca

*L*ike steak and potatoes, steak and salad greens make equal partners in a great marriage. The fatty skirt steak works well with the acid of the orange and the tart creamy zing of the blue cheese.

For lunch or a light dinner, this is one of our most popular salads.

SERVES 6

For the steak marinade:

2 pounds skirt steak
3 tablespoons fresh orange juice
2 tablespoons olive oil
2 tablespoons finely chopped fresh rosemary leaves
4 garlic cloves, minced
1½ teaspoons kosher salt
½ to 1 teaspoon black pepper

For the salad:

3 bunches watercress, well washed and torn apart
3 ounces Maytag or other blue cheese, grated or crumbled (see note)
½ pound green beans, blanched and halved
3 tablespoons extra-virgin olive oil
1½ tablespoons fresh lemon juice
¼ cup coarsely chopped walnuts (optional)

To marinate the steak: Place all the ingredients, except the salt and pepper, in a ceramic or glass bowl and stir to combine. Cover and refrigerate at least 4 hours or up to overnight.

Just before cooking the steak, prepare the salad: Divide the watercress between 4 plates and top with equal amounts of Maytag cheese and beans. Drizzle with the extra-virgin olive oil and lemon juice.

Prepare a grill.

Remove the steak from the bowl and discard the marinade. Dry with paper towels and sprinkle with the salt and pepper. Place the steak on the grill and cook until deeply browned, about 3 to 4 minutes on each side. Transfer to a cutting board and thinly slice on the diagonal. Place on the salad and sprinkle with the walnuts, if desired.

Serve immediately.

NOTE: Place the cheese in the freezer for at least 20 minutes. Put a chunk in a rotary cheese grater and grate.

SALAD DRESSINGS
and SAUCES

Herbed Goat Cheese

Great to dollop on pizza, salads, pasta, and burgers or swirl into polenta, Herbed Goat Cheese is versatile, easy to make, long lasting, and tastes great.

MAKES ABOUT 1 CUP

1 cup goat cheese or ricotta, at room temperature
1 teaspoon chopped fresh rosemary leaves
1 teaspoon chopped fresh sage leaves
1 teaspoon chopped fresh oregano leaves
Kosher salt to taste (depends on saltiness of goat cheese)
Pinch black pepper

Place all the ingredients in a small bowl and mix to combine.
Serve immediately, or cover and refrigerate up to 3 days.

Tomato, Avocado, and
Onion Salsa

*T*his is a basic salsa that is great served on the Chickpea Burger (page 190), on any basic turkey or beef burger, or on grilled swordfish or bass. If you slice the vegetables instead of dicing them, you have a great summer salad. This should be served the same day it's made.

Avocados don't ripen until after they're picked, so let them sit out at room temperature until they're perfect: they should bounce back gently when pressed. The much-maligned avocado is high in fat, but some studies indicate that moderate consumption may lower cholesterol levels.

MAKES 1½ TO 2 CUPS SALSA

½ red onion, diced
2 large beefsteak tomatoes, diced
1 ripe avocado, diced
1 tablespoon chopped fresh cilantro leaves
1 tablespoon chopped fresh basil leaves
1 tablespoon fresh lemon juice
1 tablespoon extra-virgin olive oil
½ teaspoon kosher salt

Place all the ingredients in a medium-sized mixing bowl and toss to combine. Cover and refrigerate at least 1 hour or up to 4.

Almond Pesto

I love the combo of toasty almonds and basil as opposed to the more classic pine nuts or walnuts. Spread this on pizza (page 164), toss with spaghetti, or place a dollop on a baked potato and call me on your way to heaven.

MAKES ½ TO ¾ CUP OR ENOUGH FOR TWO PIZZAS

¼ cup toasted almonds (see note)
2 garlic cloves
2 cups fresh basil leaves
6 tablespoons extra-virgin olive oil
½ teaspoon kosher salt
1 teaspoon freshly grated Parmesan cheese

Place the almonds and garlic cloves in a food processor fitted with a steel blade and pulse until they are well chopped. Add the basil and pulse until chopped. While the machine is running, gradually add the oil and process until smooth. Add the salt and Parmesan cheese and process until combined.

Use immediately, or cover and refrigerate up to 2 days.

NOTE: To toast almonds (or other nuts): Place the nuts on a large skillet over medium heat and cook, shaking or stirring occasionally, until the nuts are brown, about 3 to 5 minutes.

Quick White Bean Hummus

I've replaced the traditional chickpeas with white beans to create a lighter taste and texture. Use this as a dip for crudités or crispy crackers or as a sandwich spread with smoked ham and tomatoes.

MAKES ABOUT 1¼ CUPS

2 cups cooked white cannellini beans, rinsed and drained
3 garlic cloves, crushed or finely chopped
¼ to ½ cup water
2 tablespoons extra-virgin olive oil
3 tablespoons fresh lemon juice
½ teaspoon ground cumin, or more to taste
½ teaspoon Hungarian paprika
1 teaspoon kosher salt

Place the beans and garlic in a food processor fitted with a steel blade and process until smooth. While the machine is running, gradually add the remaining ingredients and process until smooth.

Serve immediately, or cover and refrigerate up to 3 days.

Roasted Eggplant Mediterraneo

*E*ggplants are revered in many Arab cultures, and recipes for cooking them were considered an essential part of a dowry. However, they are infamous for sponging up fats. Instead of sautéing the eggplant, we roast it, which produces an eggplant dish with a rich, smoky flavor and little fat. In addition, this technique releases some of the eggplant's bitter juices. This recipe will make you fall in love with this technique.

Roasted Eggplant Mediterraneo can be used like salsa and makes a great dip for crudités and pita toasts, or it can be used as a relish for a salmon, chicken, or beef burger. Serve with crostini, or cover a plate with a bed of greens and place a mound on top.

MAKES ABOUT 1 CUP

1 large eggplant, pricked with the tines of a fork
2 garlic cloves, finely chopped
¼ cup crumbled Bulgarian feta cheese (see note on page 43)
1 teaspoon chopped fresh oregano leaves or ⅓ teaspoon dried
1 teaspoon chopped fresh mint leaves
¼ cup fresh lemon juice
1 beefsteak tomato or 2 plum tomatoes, cored and diced
¼ cup pitted, black olives, chopped, such as Calamata, oil cured,
*   or Gaeta*
½ teaspoon kosher salt
¼ teaspoon black pepper

Preheat the oven to 450 degrees.

Place the eggplant in the oven and roast, turning often, until it is very soft when pricked with a fork, about 45 minutes. When it is cool enough to handle, scoop out the flesh, place in a large mixing bowl, and coarsely mash. Discard the skin.

Add the remaining ingredients and stir until just blended.

Transfer to a small serving bowl and serve immediately, or cover and refrigerate up to 8 hours.

Gras Pistas

I learned to make Gras Pistas from Nadia Santini in a small restaurant called Dal Pescatore in the Montava region of Italy. The time I spent in Nadia's kitchen was truly my greatest experience while working in Italy; while Nadia cooked, her mother and father helped, and her husband, Antonio, ran the front. Dal Pescatore was the kind of place where you went to the hen house when you needed an egg or to the eel pond when you needed an eel. Nadia taught me an enormous amount about the cooking of her region. She served this over grilled polenta, taking basil to a new plateau.

The Italians have pesto and Gras Pistas, and the French have pistou, all of which were probably developed as a way to preserve basil. Basically a basil and parsley pesto, Gras Pistas was originally made with lard. My version uses what today's health advocates consider more healthy—olive oil. Of course, this could all change tomorrow.

Gras Pistas is great spooned over almost anything: polenta, mashed potatoes, grilled vegetables, chicken, fish, steak, or lamb, or as a dip for focaccia.

MAKES ABOUT 1½ CUPS

5 garlic cloves
1 cup walnuts or pine nuts
½ cup chopped fresh basil leaves
1 cup chopped fresh Italian flat-leaf parsley
¼ cup chopped fresh mint leaves
½ cup extra-virgin olive oil

Place the garlic in a food processor fitted with a steel blade and pulse until coarsely chopped.

Add the walnuts and pulse. Add the basil, parsley, and mint and pulse.

While the machine is running, gradually add the oil, one tablespoon at a time, and blend until it forms a loose paste.

Use immediately, or cover and refrigerate up to 1 day.

Baba Ghanoush with Mint Oil and Lemon Zest

*T*raditional Baba Ghanoush is usually made with eggplant, tahini, garlic, lemon juice, and olive oil. I've added the refreshing, palate-cleansing taste of lemon zest and mint. Baba Ghanoush is great on crispy cracker bread.

MAKES ABOUT 1 CUP

1 large eggplant, pricked with the tines of a fork
1 tablespoon olive oil
1 garlic clove
2 tablespoons tahini (ground sesame seed paste)
2 tablespoons fresh lemon juice
1 tablespoon Mint Oil (page 34) or 1 tablespoon chopped fresh mint
     leaves
½ teaspoon kosher salt
¼ teaspoon black pepper
1 to 2 teaspoons fresh lemon zest, for garnish
¼ cup minced scallions, for garnish
¼ cup chopped fresh cilantro leaves, for garnish

Preheat the oven to 425 degrees.

To roast the eggplant: Rub the olive oil on the eggplant, transfer it to the oven, and roast, turning often, until it is very soft when pricked with a fork, about 45 minutes. For a smokier flavor, the eggplant can be grilled or cooked directly over a gas flame. Set aside to cool.

When the eggplant is cool enough to handle, scoop out the flesh and discard the skin. Place the garlic in a food processor fitted with a steel blade and pulse until finely chopped. Add the eggplant and tahini and pulse to combine.

Add the lemon juice, Mint Oil, salt, and pepper. Cover and refrigerate at least 1 hour and up to overnight.

Serve garnished with the lemon zest, scallions, and cilantro.

Two Flavored Aiolis

A mayonnaise by any other name . . . would taste just as sweet.

I'm a closet mayo lover, but I know it's not cool to like it in the '90s, so this is how I get around it.

Because of the raw egg yolk, these must be refrigerated at all times. Foods containing raw egg yolks should not be served to very young children, elderly adults, or anyone with a compromised immune system.

Mustard Aioli

We use this predominantly for the Kielbasa, Sauerkraut, and Potato Pizza (page 168), but it's also great on steamed potatoes, ham sandwiches, and grilled steak.

MAKES ABOUT 1¼ CUPS

1 garlic clove
2 tablespoons fresh lemon juice
2 large egg yolks
1 cup olive oil
1 teaspoon water
2 to 3 tablespoons Dijon mustard
½ teaspoon kosher salt
Pinch black pepper

Place the garlic in a food processor fitted with a steel blade and pulse until well chopped but not minced. Add the lemon juice and egg yolks and process until well incorporated. While the machine is running, gradually add the oil in a thin, steady stream and process until smooth. Add the water, Dijon mustard, salt, and pepper and process until thickened.

Transfer to a jar. Cover and refrigerate at least 1 hour or up to 1 day.

Basil Aioli

Great on the Portobello Burger (page 192) or the Chickpea Burger (190) or on a fresh garden-ripe tomato sandwich.

Don't be surprised when you end up with yellow aioli: this will not be green.

MAKES ABOUT 1 ¼ CUPS

1 garlic clove
2 cups fresh basil leaves
2 tablespoons fresh lemon juice
2 large egg yolks
1 cup olive oil
1 teaspoon water
½ teaspoon kosher salt
Pinch black pepper

Place the garlic and basil in a food processor fitted with a steel blade and pulse until well chopped but not minced. Add the lemon juice and egg yolks and process until well incorporated. While the machine is running, gradually add the oil in a thin, steady stream and process until smooth. Add the water, salt, and pepper and process until thickened.

Transfer to a jar. Cover and refrigerate at least 1 hour or up to 1 day.

Walnut Vinaigrette

Although we use this primarily on our Boston Bibb and watercress salad, I especially like to serve it on grilled steak, grilled pork chops, and roasted chicken. Of course, it's good on any salad with any kind of blue cheese, garnished with additional walnuts.

MAKES ABOUT 1 CUP

¼ cup fresh lemon juice
2 tablespoons balsamic vinegar
1 teaspoon chopped fresh sage leaves
1 teaspoon chopped fresh oregano leaves
1 teaspoon chopped fresh thyme leaves
1 to 2 garlic cloves
½ teaspoon kosher salt
¼ teaspoon black pepper
¼ cup toasted walnuts (see note on page 67)
½ cup extra-virgin olive oil

Place the lemon juice, vinegar, sage, oregano, thyme, garlic, salt, pepper, and 2 tablespoons walnuts in a blender and blend until combined. While the machine is running, gradually add the oil and blend until emulsified. Use immediately, or cover and refrigerate up to 5 days.

When using on a salad, garnish with the remaining 2 tablespoons walnuts.

Lemon Vinaigrette

I may be putting myself on the line here, but there are a few very specific things I judge all cooks by: their ability to make and understand bread, desserts, and a simple vinaigrette. A good cook always knows how to balance flavors, and the ratio of oil to acid is critical. Hopefully, you'll judge me well on this one.

MAKES ABOUT 1½ CUPS

½ cup fresh lemon juice
1 cup extra-virgin olive oil
1 garlic clove, minced
½ teaspoon chopped fresh sage leaves (optional)
½ teaspoon fresh thyme leaves (optional)
¼ teaspoon kosher salt
⅛ teaspoon black pepper

Place all the ingredients in a blender and blend until smooth. Transfer to a jar. Cover and refrigerate at least 1 hour or up to 2 days.

Balsamic Shallot Vinaigrette

earty balsamic vinegar is rich and pungent, and it's chocolatey aroma makes it a delicious accent drizzled on mesclun greens, particularly bitter ones like endive, radicchio, watercress, or arugula.

I also love to drizzle this on grilled steak, roast chicken, or dead-ripe August tomatoes.

MAKES ABOUT ⅓ TO ½ CUP,
ENOUGH TO DRESS A SALAD FOR 4

*¼ cup chopped slab bacon, or 2 slices, chopped
1 shallot, minced
1 small garlic clove, minced
3 tablespoons balsamic vinegar
3 tablespoons extra-virgin olive oil
Pinch kosher salt
Pinch black pepper*

Place a small skillet over medium-high heat and, when it is hot, add the bacon. Cook until it is rendered of fat and drain off all but 1 teaspoon. Add the shallot and garlic and cook until lightly golden. Add the vinegar, oil, salt, and pepper. Bring to a simmer and cook until it coats the back of a spoon.

Use immediately, or cover and refrigerate up to 3 days.

Variation

Add 1 teaspoon Dijon mustard and/or 1 tablespoon honey when you add the oil.

Crumbled Roquefort Dressing

*B*ecause Roquefort is my all-time favorite cheese, I can't resist just dipping bread into this dressing. For those more disciplined, I recommend serving it on green salads or grilled steak or on a salad of sliced tomatoes and raw red onions, steakhouse style.

Feel free to substitute your favorite kind of blue-veined cheese.

MAKES ABOUT 1½ CUPS

2½ tablespoons red wine vinegar
1 tablespoon fresh lemon juice
¼ cup extra-virgin olive oil
¼ cup olive oil
½ teaspoon salt
¼ teaspoon pepper
1 cup crumbled Roquefort cheese
1 shallot, minced

Place the vinegar, lemon juice, oils, salt, and pepper in a small mixing bowl and mix until well combined. Add the Roquefort cheese and shallot and mix well.

Use immediately, or cover and refrigerate up to 3 days.

Caesar Salad Dressing

I heavily resisted putting this recipe in this book. Although it's a common American classic, it has little to do with anything Italian or Mediterranean, but I humbly admit to loving it. When it is poured on the innermost leaves of Romaine, and garnished with croutons and shaved Parmesan, there is nothing quite like it.

The secret to this dressing, which is eggless, is to have all the ingredients ice cold when you start. The best way to do that is to refrigerate everything beforehand. Do not let anything get warm, or the dressing will break and separate. If it gets too thick, simply blend in an ice cube.

MAKES ABOUT 1¼ TO 1½ CUPS

3 garlic cloves
3 anchovy fillets
½ cup fresh lemon juice, chilled (about 2 lemons)
1 teaspoon Dijon mustard
1 teaspoon dry mustard
6 tablespoons freshly grated Parmesan cheese, chilled
1 to 1¼ cups canola or vegetable oil, chilled
½ teaspoon kosher salt
¼ teaspoon black pepper

Place the garlic and anchovies in a blender or the bowl of a food processor fitted with a steel blade, and pulse until minced. Add the lemon juice and mustards and pulse until combined.

While the machine is running, gradually add the Parmesan cheese, oil, salt, and pepper.

Serve immediately, or cover and refrigerate up to 3 days.

SOUPS

Mushroom Minestrone

*M*inestrone will always top my list of great soups. I have the fondest memories of minestrone because I've tasted too many bad versions; but when you do it right, it's the stuff of good memories. The mushrooms, which seem so natural here, add an earthiness to this already complex soup.

Minestrone, like all the soups in this chapter, partners beautifully with a green salad and a hunk of Tuscan bread to make a complete meal.

MAKES ABOUT 10 TO 12 CUPS

2 tablespoons olive oil
2 cups button mushrooms, trimmed and sliced
2 cups shiitake mushrooms, trimmed and sliced
2 portobello mushrooms, trimmed and sliced
1 cup chopped slab bacon (optional)
1 ham hock (optional)
1 Spanish onion, chopped
½ head fennel, diced
2 garlic cloves, thinly sliced
1 carrot, peeled, if desired, and diced
1 celery stalk, diced
¼ head Savoy cabbage, cored and chopped
1½ cups chopped canned tomatoes, drained
8 cups Chicken Broth (page 40) or canned low-sodium chicken broth
1½ teaspoons chopped fresh rosemary leaves
Shaved Parmesan cheese, for garnish
Fresh chopped basil leaves, for garnish
Almond Pesto (optional), for garnish (page 67)

Place a large skillet over high heat and, when it is hot, add 1 tablespoon oil. Add 2 cups mushrooms and cook until they are well seared, about 4 minutes. Repeat, adding about 2 cups at a time, until all the mushrooms are cooked. Set aside.

Place a large stockpot over medium-high heat and, when it is hot, add the remaining 1 tablespoon oil. Add the bacon, if desired, and cook until it is just crisp, about 3 to 5 minutes. Add the ham hock, if desired, onion, fennel, garlic, carrot, celery, and cabbage, stirring well after each addition, and cook until wilted, about 5 minutes. Add the reserved mushrooms, tomatoes, Chicken Broth, and rosemary and cook for 1½ hours.

Transfer 6 cups of the soup to the blender or a food processor fitted with a steel blade and process until smooth. Return the purée to the stockpot and cook for 30 minutes.

Cover and refrigerate up to 2 days, or serve immediately by placing a big hunk of Tuscan bread in a shallow bowl and pouring the minestrone over it. Garnish with Parmesan cheese, chopped basil, and, if desired, Almond Pesto.

White Bean Soup

$\mathcal{W}$hite beans rule! White beans, the poor man's gourmet food, have so much character they can play many roles. When I'm really hungry for something wholesome and heartwarming, I reach for white beans. This quick, nutritious, and easy soup is perfect for dinner served with a loaf of Tuscan-style bread, a great salad, and a glass of red wine.

MAKES ABOUT 8 CUPS

2 tablespoons olive oil

1 carrot, peeled, if desired, and finely diced

1 Spanish onion, peeled and diced

3 garlic cloves, chopped

2 celery stalks, diced

1 fennel bulb, cut in small dice

1 ham hock (optional)

1 teaspoon dried fennel seed

1 tablespoon chopped fresh rosemary leaves or 1 teaspoon dried

¼ teaspoon crushed red pepper flakes

1 teaspoon kosher salt

½ teaspoon black pepper

1 head Roasted Garlic (page 28), peeled

2 cups cooked white cannellini beans, rinsed and drained

6 cups Chicken Broth (page 40) or canned low-sodium chicken broth

1 bunch escarole or bunch spinach, well washed and torn apart

Place a large stockpot over medium heat and, when it is hot, add the oil. Add the carrot, onion, garlic, celery, fennel, ham hock, if desired, fennel seed, rosemary, red pepper flakes, salt, and pepper and cook until the vegetables become translucent, about 5 to 10 minutes.

Add the Roasted Garlic, beans, and Chicken Broth and raise the heat to high. Bring to a boil and lower the heat to low. Simmer, uncovered, for 20 minutes.

Place half the soup in a blender or food processor fitted with a steel blade and pulse until the mixture is thick but not completely smooth. Return it to the stockpot.

Add the escarole or spinach, if desired, and cook until wilted. Serve immediately, cover and refrigerate up to 3 days, or freeze up to 3 weeks.

Roasted Vegetable Soup

his rich vegetable soup gets its intense flavor from the roasted vegetables. If you try this soup without roasting the vegetables and sauté them instead, you will not achieve the same results.

Mild and buttery Savoy cabbages are the only cabbages I like or use. They are a great source of vitamin C.

For a smooth soup, omit the beans and spinach and process in a blender until creamy.

MAKES ABOUT 10 CUPS

2 to 3 parsnips, peeled, if desired, quartered lengthwise, and chopped
4 carrots, peeled, if desired, quartered lengthwise, and chopped
1 large red onion, chopped
1 head Savoy cabbage, cored and cut into eighths
8 fresh plum tomatoes (you can used canned tomatoes if fresh are not
    available)
2 tablespoons olive oil
1 teaspoon kosher salt
½ teaspoon black pepper
2 garlic cloves, minced
2 celery stalks, finely chopped
2 cups cooked white cannellini beans, rinsed and drained
6 cups Chicken Broth (page 40) or canned low-sodium chicken broth
1 bunch leaf spinach, well washed and chopped
Shaved Parmesan cheese, for garnish

Preheat the oven to 375 degrees.

Place the parsnips, carrots, onion, cabbage, and tomatoes in separate piles on a large roasting pan and drizzle with 1 tablespoon oil. Sprinkle with the salt and pepper.

Place the pan in the oven and roast for about 45 minutes, checking occasionally and removing any vegetables as they brown. Do not allow them to burn.

Place a large stockpot over medium heat and, when it is hot, add the remaining 1 tablespoon oil. Add the garlic and celery and cook until they are golden, about 3 minutes.

Roughly chop the cabbage and tomatoes and add them to the stockpot. Add the remaining vegetables, beans, and Chicken Broth. Bring to a boil. Lower the heat and simmer, uncovered, for 20 minutes.

Add the spinach.

Serve immediately, garnished with the shaved Parmesan cheese, or cover and refrigerate up to 2 days.

Tomato and Spinach Soup

*T*he Italians are ingenious in making things go a little further, using what they have—or in some cases—what they have not.

When I was in Italy, I learned the technique of thickening soups with a little semolina. It adds great texture, an interesting toasty flavor, and a complexity that lingers on your palate for a long time.

Only use leaf spinach, not the curly variety, in this soup, and be sure to wash it thoroughly to remove all grittiness; otherwise, it will ruin the soup.

MAKES ABOUT 8 CUPS

1 tablespoon olive oil
2 garlic cloves, chopped
6 plum tomatoes, chopped
4 bunches leaf spinach, well washed and coarsely chopped
½ teaspoon kosher salt
½ teaspoon pepper
4 cups Chicken Broth (page 40) or canned low-sodium chicken broth
½ cup semolina
¼ cup freshly grated Parmesan cheese
Shaved Parmesan cheese, for garnish

Place a large skillet over medium-high heat and, when it is hot, add the oil. Add the garlic and cook until lightly toasted, about 3 minutes. Add the tomatoes and cook until seared, about 3 minutes. Add the spinach and cook until wilted, about 1 minute. Add the salt, pepper, Chicken Broth, and semolina, stirring well after each addition, and bring to a boil.

Stir in the grated Parmesan cheese, and serve immediately, garnished with the shaved Parmesan cheese.

Lemony Chicken Soup with Shreds of Egg White

*B*ecause I like to work out with weights, I am always looking for ways to get more protein and less fat without sacrificing flavor. I think that this Asian-inspired soup, a cross between egg drop, avgolemono, and chicken noodle, achieves that.

To get the egg drop–like shreds, get the soup up to a high boil, add the egg whites, and stir quickly, breaking them up with a whisk as you stir. You can substitute rice for the orzo.

MAKES 12 TO 14 CUPS

2 tablespoons olive oil
2 whole boneless, skinless chicken breasts, trimmed of excess fat and
    cut in medium dice
4 garlic cloves, chopped
½ teaspoon kosher salt
½ teaspoon black pepper
1 small leek, chopped
1 small Spanish onion, chopped
1 carrot, peeled, if desired, and chopped
½ fennel bulb, chopped
8 large egg whites
½ to ¾ cup fresh lemon juice
6 to 8 cups Chicken Broth (page 40) or canned low-sodium
    chicken broth
½ cup orzo
⅓ to ½ cup freshly grated Parmesan cheese
2 tablespoons chopped fresh parsley leaves, for garnish
2 tablespoons chopped fresh basil leaves, for garnish

Place a large stockpot over medium heat and, when it is hot, add the oil. Add the chicken and cook until it just begins to turn white, about 2 minutes. Add the garlic, salt, pepper, leek, onion, carrot, and fennel, stirring well after each addition, and cook until the vegetables are soft, about 10 minutes.

Place the egg whites and lemon juice in a small bowl, mix to combine and set aside.

Add the Chicken Broth and bring to a boil. Add the orzo and cook until tender, about 8 to 10 minutes. Quickly whisk in the egg lemon mixture, stirring all the while. Add the Parmesan cheese and stir to combine.

Serve immediately, garnished with the parsley and basil.

Fall Potato Soup
with Cauliflower and Duck

$\mathcal{A}$lthough people always love this soup, I have trouble selling it because when customers hear cauliflower, they think about the damage their mothers did to that much-maligned vegetable when they were growing up. Overcooked, stinky cauliflower this is not: this soup is earthy, smooth, and rich, and when we don't sell it all, I'm happy to get a big bowl for myself at the end of the night.

You can completely eliminate the duck legs from this recipe or substitute chicken legs. If you are not using either, reduce the cooking time to 45 minutes. You can also add a ham hock for a smoky flavor.

MAKES 12 CUPS

2 tablespoons olive oil
4 duck legs, skinned (optional)
1 teaspoon kosher salt
½ teaspoon black pepper
1 Spanish onion, chopped
3 to 4 garlic cloves, chopped
1½ heads cauliflower, cored and cut into florets
2 Idaho potatoes, cubed
2 tablespoons chopped fresh rosemary leaves
6 to 8 cups Chicken Broth (page 40) or canned low-sodium
  chicken broth

Preheat the oven to 375 degrees.

Place a large shallow ovenproof pot over medium-high heat and, when it is hot, add 1 tablespoon oil. Add the duck legs, salt, and pepper and cook for 2 minutes. Add the onion and garlic and cook until the garlic is toasted, about 3 minutes. Add the cauliflower, potatoes, and rosemary and cook 3 to 4 minutes. Add the

Chicken Broth and bring to a boil. Cover and place in the oven until the duck falls off the bone, about 2 hours.

Remove the duck, place on a plate, and shred. Transfer the soup, in batches, to a blender and purée. Pass through a sieve or a strainer and discard the solids.

Place a small skillet over medium-high heat and, when it is hot, add the remaining 1 tablespoon oil. Add the duck and cook until lightly browned, about 3 to 4 minutes.

Place the soup in shallow bowls and serve immediately, topped with the shredded duck.

Wild Mushroom Ribollita

Ribollita is a traditional Florentine bean soup made with vegetables, bread, and cheese, and there are as many renditions as there are cooks. In my frustrated search to buy Tuscan Black Cabbage, the essential ingredient in true *ribollita*, I abandoned all preconceived notions about what it is supposed to be and decided to do my own version entirely. I threw out the vegetables and beans and substituted mushrooms instead. It's become a staple that we serve as an accompaniment to roasted chicken and grilled fish.

MAKES ABOUT 10 CUPS

2 tablespoons olive oil

3 to 4 garlic cloves, thinly sliced

2 onions, thinly sliced

½ pound button mushrooms, trimmed and sliced

¾ pound shiitake mushrooms, trimmed (about 2½ cups)

½ pound oyster mushrooms, trimmed and chopped

3 ounces fresh or 1½ ounces dried porcini mushrooms

½ pound portobello mushrooms, including the stem, chopped

1 Idaho potato, diced

1 tablespoon chopped fresh rosemary leaves

6 cups Chicken Broth (page 40) or canned low-sodium chicken broth

3 cups bread cubes

½ cup freshly grated Parmesan cheese

2 balls (4 ounces each) buffalo mozzarella cheese, chopped

2 tomatoes, diced, for garnish

½ cup chopped fresh basil leaves, for garnish

Place a large stockpot over medium-high heat and, when it is hot, add the oil. Add the garlic and onion and cook until the garlic is toasted, about 3 minutes. Add

the mushrooms, potato, and rosemary and cook until the mushrooms have softened, about 20 minutes. Add the Chicken Broth and bring to a boil. Lower the heat and cook for 1 hour.

Add the bread cubes, Parmesan cheese, and mozzarella cheese and stir to melt the cheeses. Place in shallow bowls and serve immediately, garnished with the tomato and basil.

Black Bean Chili

I developed this chili to serve on top of chicken hot dogs, but it's great served alone, accompanied by Cucumber Salad (page 51). For a heartier meal, serve it with Polenta (page 132) or Sweet Potato Polenta (page 134).

Black beans are extremely underrated, but I like their depth and complexity of flavor and adaptability. When I was growing up, chili was a Sunday afternoon, college football–watching staple. As soon as there's a nip in the air, I look forward to watching football and eating chili with my oldest son, Oliver. Ingesting and digesting heavy beef chili was no easy feat week after week; this version is substantially lighter and easier on the stomach.

This makes about 12 cups of chili, and if you don't need it all (unless you're having a Superbowl party), it freezes well.

MAKES ABOUT 12 CUPS

1 teaspoon olive oil
1 Spanish onion, minced
4 garlic cloves, minced
1 pound ground turkey
2 jalapeño peppers, finely chopped
6 cups diced fresh or canned tomatoes
1 teaspoon Dijon mustard
1 teaspoon ground cumin
1 teaspoon chili powder
4 cups cooked black beans, rinsed and drained
½ to 1 cup Chicken Broth (page 40) or water, if necessary
2 tablespoons balsamic vinegar
1 teaspoon kosher salt
½ teaspoon black pepper
Juice of 1 lime

4 scallions, chopped, for garnish
⅓ to ½ cup chopped fresh cilantro leaves, for garnish

Place a large nonstick stockpot over medium heat and, when it is hot, add the oil. Add the onion and garlic and cook until the onion is translucent, about 4 minutes.

Add the turkey, jalapeño, tomatoes, mustard, cumin, and chili powder and cook for 4 minutes. Stir occasionally, breaking up the turkey with the back of a wooden spoon. Add the beans and cook, uncovered, for about 45 minutes, adding Chicken Broth or water if it becomes too thick.

Add the vinegar, salt, and pepper and cook for 5 minutes. Just prior to serving, add the lime juice.

Serve immediately, garnished with the scallions and cilantro, or cover and refrigerate up to 3 days.

Chilled Tomato and Cucumber Soup

 ormer Figs chef Sarah Jenkins helped develop this easy, refreshing, and delicious soup, though because of the lavish use of olive oil, neither Sally nor my wife, Olivia, felt that this recipe should be included in this cookbook, or for that matter, exist. Rich it may be, but customers won't let me take it off the Figs menu, especially in the hot summer months. So here it is: feel free to reduce the amount of olive oil as you see fit . . . but if you do, don't say it's my recipe.

MAKES 5 TO 6 CUPS

2 slicing cucumbers, peeled, seeded, and cut in eighths
12 perfect plum tomatoes, cored and quartered
2 cups extra virgin-olive oil
2 tablespoons sherry vinegar
1 tablespoon kosher salt
2 teaspoons black pepper
Toasted sesame seeds, for garnish

Place all the ingredients, except the toasted sesame seeds, in a blender and purée. Pour through a strainer and discard the solids. Cover and refrigerate at least 2 hours or up to overnight.

Divide among 6 shallow bowls and garnish with the toasted sesame seeds.

BASIC SAUCES *for* PIZZA, PASTA, *and* POLENTA

Portobello and Shiitake Mushroom Ragù

I love mushrooms, and so do my customers at both Olives and Figs. Traditionally, a ragù is an Italian meat sauce, so it's not technically correct to call this a ragù, but the portobello mushrooms have such a substantial flavor and texture that you almost can't tell there's no meat in the sauce.

You can make this ahead of time, if you want, up to the last step. When you're ready to eat it, add the butter. Be sure to use veal or beef broth: this recipe does not work well with chicken broth. Serve on top of Polenta (page 132) or any kind of noodle.

MAKES ABOUT 1 TO 1½ CUPS

1½ teaspoons olive oil
2 portobello mushroom caps, trimmed and sliced
1 cup shiitake mushrooms, trimmed
1 garlic clove, thinly sliced
¾ cup tomatoes, drained and chopped
2 tablespoons red wine
2 tablespoons veal or beef broth
1 tablespoon unsalted butter
Shaved Parmesan cheese, for garnish

Place a large cast-iron skillet over high heat and, when it is hot, add ½ teaspoon oil. Add the mushroom caps and cook until they are seared, about 3 to 5 minutes. Set aside. Add the shiitake mushrooms and cook until they are seared, about 3 minutes. Set aside.

Reheat the skillet and add the remaining 1 teaspoon oil. Add the garlic and cook until it is lightly toasted, about 2 to 3 minutes. Add the tomatoes and red wine and cook for 2 minutes. Add the broth and cook for 2 to 3 minutes. Add the reserved mushrooms and cook until the liquid lightly coats the back of a spoon, about 7 to 10 minutes.

Add the butter and stir.

Serve immediately, garnished with the Parmesan cheese, or cover and refrigerate up to 2 days.

Sweet and Savory
Sausage Sauce

*I*f you don't want to use pork sausage, substitute turkey or chicken sausage or a combination. You can use regular tomatoes, but using Roasted Tomatoes (page 32) adds a lovely sweetness. This potent sauce can be used on any medium-sized shaped pasta like oriechette, shells, rotini, or on Polenta (page 132).

MAKES 5 TO 6 CUPS

1 pound garlic sausage, taken out of casing and crumbled

3 to 4 garlic cloves, chopped

2 teaspoons chopped fresh rosemary leaves

2 teaspoons fresh thyme leaves

1 Spanish onion, chopped

1 cup white wine

*3 cups homemade or low-sodium canned veal, beef, or chicken broth
    (see Chicken Broth, page 40)*

2 anchovy fillets, finely chopped

Two 28-ounce cans whole plum tomatoes, drained and hand crushed

1 tablespoon unsalted butter (optional)

Place a large skillet or stockpot over medium-high heat and, when it is hot, add the sausage. When the fat begins to render, add the garlic and 1 teaspoon each rosemary and thyme and cook until lightly toasted, about 2 minutes. Discard any excess fat. Add the onion, lower the heat to low, and cook until it is almost caramelized, about 15 to 20 minutes.

Add the wine to deglaze the pan. Add the broth, and cook until reduced to a thick syrup, about 5 to 8 minutes. Add the anchovies and tomatoes and the remaining 1 teaspoon each of rosemary and thyme, and cook until the flavors meld together, about 20 to 30 minutes. Add the butter, if desired.

Serve immediately, or cover and refrigerate up to 3 days.

Basic Tomato Sauce

Our standard pizza and spaghetti sauce.

Let's talk about tomato sauce: I don't know why it is so bad so often. I have dreadful memories of the school cafeteria tomato sauce loaded with green peppers, sugar, and tomato paste. What would make somebody think of putting a sauce like this together? No. No. No. Simple and fresh is best. Buy the best possible ingredients (keeping in mind that fresh tomatoes are not always as good as canned because the tomatoes have to be canned when they're perfectly ripe). Don't add too many flavors. Don't overdo it.

In Italy, I've even seen some pizza tomato sauces where they simply crush the tomatoes in their hands, pour olive oil over the top, add a little chopped garlic, salt, and pepper, and then tear some fresh basil over it and place it on a pizza to cook.

MAKES ABOUT 1½ QUARTS

1 tablespoon olive or vegetable oil
2 to 3 garlic cloves, minced
½ cup red wine
1 tablespoon dried Greek oregano
One 28-ounce can diced tomatoes
One 28-ounce can whole tomatoes in juice
1 cup Chicken Broth (page 40) or water
2½ tablespoons fresh basil leaves, coarsely chopped
½ to 2 teaspoons kosher salt
½ teaspoon black pepper

Place a large saucepan over medium heat and, when it is hot, add the oil. Add the garlic and cook until lightly toasted, about 2 to 3 minutes. Add the wine to deglaze the pan and cook until reduced by about a third, about 5 minutes.

Add the oregano, tomatoes, and Chicken Broth and cook, stirring occasionally, for 5 minutes. Lower the heat to low and cook until the mixture starts to come together as a sauce, about 45 minutes. Add the basil, salt, and pepper.

Serve immediately, or cover and refrigerate up to 3 days.

Roasted Tomato Sauce

This may sound more complicated than the Basic Tomato Sauce (page 105), but it's actually even simpler to make and richer in flavor.

MAKES 3 TO 3½ CUPS

3 pounds fresh plum tomatoes or two 28-ounce cans plum tomatoes,
*   well drained*
½ cup Chicken Broth (page 40) or water
1 large Spanish onion, sliced
½ cup whole fresh basil leaves
⅓ cup canola or olive oil
2 teaspoons kosher salt
½ to 1 teaspoon black pepper

Preheat the oven to 375 degrees.

Place all the ingredients in a roasting pan and toss to combine. Transfer to the oven and cook until the tomato skins are charred and the sauce has begun to come together, 45 minutes to 1 hour. Coarsely chop the tomato, taking care to scrape up pan juices.

Serve immediately, or cover and refrigerate up to 3 days.

Calabrese Sauce

*M*y great-grandparents came from a small village in Calabria, and I have wonderful memories of my great-great-grandmother, Bettina, standing over the stove stirring this sauce. What I particularly love is that she passed it down to my grandmother who passed it down to my mother who passed it down to me. I call it Calabrese in their honor.

This sauce often is called gravy: a little less tomatoey than others, it was probably devised because of the unavailability of good-quality tomatoes. It is a sauce that was meant to be stretched in households without means.

We use it primarily for pasta and polenta. You can also do as the Italians do: pull the meat out, serve the remaining tomato sauce as a starter on pasta, and eat the meat as the entrée.

MAKES ABOUT 10 CUPS

¼ cup all-purpose flour

1 teaspoon kosher salt

½ teaspoon black pepper

½ pound pork shoulder, cut in 1½- to 2-inch cubes

¼ pound beef shoulder or rump, cut in small dice

¼ pound veal shoulder or breast, cut in small dice

1 tablespoon olive oil

1 large Spanish onion, diced

4 garlic cloves, minced

1 carrot, peeled, if desired, and diced

1 celery stalk, diced

4 anchovy fillets, minced

1½ tablespoons dried Greek oregano

½ cup red wine

One 28-ounce can diced tomatoes

One 28-ounce can whole plum tomatoes in juice

1½ tablespoons fresh oregano leaves

Place the flour, salt, and pepper on a large plate and lightly dredge the pork, beef, and veal.

Place a large skillet or Dutch oven over medium-low heat and, when it is hot, add the oil. Add the pork, beef, and veal and sear it, in batches, until you get a light color. Do not let it brown. Set the meat aside and discard all but 1 tablespoon fat.

Add the onion, garlic, carrot, and celery and cook until softened but not browned, about 5 minutes. Add the anchovy fillets and dried oregano and stir. Add the wine to the skillet. Deglaze and cook until reduced by half, about 10 minutes. Add the reserved meat and the tomatoes and cook for 5 minutes. Do not let it boil. Lower the heat to low and cook until thickened, about 1 hour and 15 minutes. Add the fresh oregano and cook for 15 minutes.

Serve immediately, or cover and refrigerate up to 3 days.

Portobello, Porcini, and Button Mushroom Purée

*E*arthy, rich, and intense, this purée is great to keep around to swirl into risotto, toss with spaghetti, or serve under a roasted chicken breast or a grilled steak.

Don't omit the porcini mushrooms. Most specialty stores sell them dried.

MAKES ABOUT 1 CUP

1 tablespoon olive oil
2 teaspoons chopped garlic
½ cup sliced Spanish onion
¼ cup red wine
4 portobello mushroom caps, trimmed and coarsely chopped
(about 1½ cups)
¼ cup dried or frozen porcini mushrooms, coarsely chopped (soaked and
strained, if dried)
½ cup button mushrooms, trimmed and coarsely chopped
¼ to ½ teaspoon kosher salt
1 teaspoon chopped fresh rosemary leaves
¼ to ½ cup heavy cream

Place a large skillet over medium heat and, when it is hot, add the oil. Add the garlic and onion and cook until translucent, about 3 to 5 minutes. Add the wine to deglaze the skillet.

Add the mushrooms and cook until soft, about 8 to 10 minutes. Add the salt, rosemary, and cream and cook until slightly reduced, about 3 to 4 minutes. Transfer to a food processor fitted with a steel blade and pulse until it has the consistency of thick mud.

Serve immediately, or cover and refrigerate up to one week.

PASTA

Macaroni Simoni

*N*amed after my two-year old son, Simon, Macaroni Simoni is what macaroni and cheese is supposed to be: subtle and creamy but cheesy and intense. It's more like a children's alfredo sauce than what you'd expect to find in a box.

I thought about not including it because the secret ingredient, powdered cheddar cheese, isn't available in grocery stores and can only be purchased by mail order. If you're thinking that it's some nasty synthetic product, don't turn your nose up so fast: It's simply cheddar cheese without any water content, and it's also great sprinkled on popcorn and broccoli. (Cabot Creamery 1-800-453-8927.)

If you want to prepare this ahead, assemble the ingredients, cover with aluminum foil, and refrigerate. Bake at 350 degrees, about 10 minutes. Remove the foil, raise the heat to 400, and bake until bubbly and slightly browned, about 7 to 10 minutes more.

SERVES 6 TO 8

1 pound orzo or small shells
¼ cup unsalted butter
¼ cup all-purpose flour
3 cups milk
¼ cup Cabot cheddar cheese powder
¼ to ⅓ cup freshly grated Parmesan cheese (do not substitute Romano)
¼ to ⅓ cup freshly grated mozzarella cheese
¼ to ⅓ cup freshly grated Italian Fontina cheese
½ cup heavy cream
½ to 1 teaspoon kosher salt
¼ teaspoon black pepper
½ to ¾ cup dry bread crumbs

Preheat the oven to 400 degrees. Lightly butter a 2-quart baking or casserole dish.

Bring a large pot of water to a boil over high heat. Add the orzo or shells and cook until *al dente*. Drain and set aside.

Place the butter in a large skillet over medium heat and cook until browned, about 2 minutes. Add the flour and cook, stirring constantly, until it loses its rawness, about 2 minutes.

Place the milk in a small saucepan and warm it over medium heat. Add ½ cup milk to the butter mixture and cook, stirring constantly, until it forms a slurry, about 1 to 2 minutes. Add the slurry to the milk and cook, stirring constantly, until thickened, about 1 to 2 minutes.

Add the powdered cheese to the milk and mix well. Add the orzo, Parmesan, mozzarella, and Fontina cheeses, cream, salt, and pepper, and mix to combine.

Transfer to the prepared dish. Sprinkle the bread crumbs on top and transfer to the oven. Bake until bubbly and slightly browned, about 7 to 10 minutes.

Serve immediately, or cover and refrigerate up to 3 days.

Lasagna

$\mathcal{T}$his recipe makes two 8 x 8 pans of lasagna because, although lasagna is definitely better the second day, it's hard to resist eating it the day you make it. I recommend the Del Verde No–Boil Lasagna Noodles because they taste great, require no time to cook, and even come with their own pans. If you want to make one big lasagna, simply make the whole recipe in a 9 x 12 pan. You will probably have leftover noodles either way.

You can use any kind of sausage you like; we've tried spicy chicken sausage for a lighter, spicier lasagna, but feel free to experiment with one sausage or a combination of several.

SERVES 12

For the sauce:

1 tablespoon olive oil

5 garlic cloves, thinly sliced

1 small Spanish onion, chopped

1½ pounds sweet or spicy Italian sausage or a combination, taken out of casing and crumbled

6 cups canned diced tomatoes

½ cup chopped fresh basil leaves

½ to 1 teaspoon kosher salt

½ teaspoon black pepper

1 package Del Verde No–Boil Lasagna Noodles

1½ pounds fresh mozzarella cheese, cut in large dice

¾ pound Italian Fontina cheese, thinly sliced

⅔ pound part–skim ricotta cheese

1 bunch fresh basil

2 teaspoons kosher salt

1 teaspoon black pepper

1 to 1½ cups freshly grated Parmesan cheese

To make the sauce:

Place a large skillet or saucepan over medium heat and, when it is hot, add the oil. Add the garlic and cook until it is toasted, about 3 to 4 minutes. Add the onion and cook until golden, about 3 to 4 minutes. Add the sausage and cook until the fat is rendered, about 10 minutes. Add the salt and pepper. Discard any excess fat.

Add the tomatoes and cook for 30 minutes. Add the basil and cook until the mixture begins to thicken, about 10 minutes.

To assemble the lasagna:

Preheat the oven to 400 degrees.

Fill a large bowl with very hot water, dip the noodles in and drain.

Cover the bottom of both pans with noodles. Spread about ¾ cup sauce in each pan. Top with about ½ cup mozzarella cheese. It does not need to cover completely. Top with 3 slices Fontina cheese. It does not need to cover completely. Top with about ¼ cup ricotta cheese, in dollops. Place about 4 basil leaves on top. Sprinkle lightly with the Parmesan cheese, salt, and pepper. Repeat 5 times. Top with a thin layer of tomato sauce and then sprinkle lightly with Parmesan cheese, salt, and pepper.

Transfer to the oven and bake until golden brown and bubbling, about 45 minutes to 1 hour.

Serve immediately, or cover and refrigerate up to 3 days.

To reheat, cover and place in a 350 degree oven, and cook until heated through, about 30 to 40 minutes.

Semolina Gnocchi à la Romano

*S*emolina makes me happy. Whether polenta or gnocchi, it goes way beyond comfort food. Homey, rich, soft, luscious, and dreamy—even mashed potatoes pale in comparison.

SERVES 6 TO 8

4 cups milk
1¼ cups semolina
½ cup heavy cream
½ cup coarsely grated Parmesan cheese
1 teaspoon kosher salt
½ teaspoon black pepper
1 tablespoon unsalted butter
½ cup diced Virginia baked ham
2 garlic cloves, chopped
½ Spanish onion, chopped
½ head Savoy cabbage, cored and thinly sliced
1 cup Chicken Broth (page 40) or canned low-sodium chicken broth
1 tablespoon chopped rosemary leaves
4 ounces Italian Gorgonzola cheese
2 tablespoons freshly grated Parmesan cheese
2 tablespoons heavy cream
1 teaspoon kosher salt
½ teaspoon black pepper

Lightly grease a 9 x 12 pan.

To make the semolina gnocchi: Place the milk in a medium saucepan over medium-high heat, bring to a boil, and slowly whisk in the semolina, continuing to whisk until it has thickened, about 2 minutes. Add the cream, Parmesan cheese, salt, and pepper and mix well. Pour into the prepared pan and smooth out with a knife or spatula. Cover with plastic wrap and refrigerate at least 1 hour or overnight. Cut out 12 circles with a biscuit cutter or the rim of a glass and set aside.

To prepare the cabbage: Place a large skillet over medium heat and, when it is hot, add the butter. Add the ham, garlic, onion, and cabbage, stirring well after each addition, and cook for 3 minutes. Add the Chicken Broth and cook until the cabbage is wilted, about 20 minutes. Add the rosemary and cook for 2 minutes.

Transfer to the prepared pan. Place the semolina circles on top of the cabbage in a circular pattern. Top with the Gorgonzola and Parmesan cheeses, drizzle with the cream, and sprinkle with the salt and pepper. Place in the oven and bake until bubbly and browned, about 15 minutes.

Serve immediately.

Couscous Carbonara with Country Ham

*C*arbonara usually refers to the brown pieces of bacon that accumulate in this sauce, the little chunks of, yes, carbon. Carbonara is traditionally made with bacon, eggs, Parmesan cheese, and cream, but I've made the egg an optional topping instead of part of the sauce, added some spinach (and then some might say it was Carbonara Florentine), and substituted Israeli couscous for the pasta. Although this can be made with orzo or any kind of tiny pasta, I think the Israeli couscous, which is available in specialty food stores, has the best texture: firm and yet delicate.

You can serve this with a poached egg and shaved truffles for a truly luxurious experience.

SERVES 4

1 tablespoon olive oil
1 garlic clove, thinly sliced
½ pound leaf spinach, well washed
⅓ cup heavy cream
1 tablespoon unsalted butter
1½ cups diced Virginia baked ham
1 pound Israeli "toasted Pasta" couscous, cooked according to
    package instructions
½ to 1 cup freshly grated Parmesan cheese

Place a large skillet over medium-high heat and, when it is hot, add the oil. Add the garlic and cook until it is lightly toasted, about 3 minutes. Add the spinach and cook until wilted, about 2 to 3 minutes. Discard the excess liquid, transfer the mixture to a blender, and blend, gradually adding the cream.

Reheat the skillet and when it is hot, add the butter. Add the ham and cook for 2 minutes. Add the reserved spinach purée and cook for 1 minute.

Add the couscous and Parmesan cheese, mix to combine, and serve immediately.

Fedelini with Braised Baby Zucchini

Although this looks too easy to include in a cookbook, it's so simple, it's easy to screw up. If you can't find baby zucchini, simply quarter regular zucchini lengthwise and then slice it thinly.

Zucchini can be overused; still it is one of my favorite vegetables. Don't worry about overcooking: It gets better as you stew it and becomes a pulpy sauce with a sensuous mouth feel. Don't be afraid of the amount of olive oil; this is the way the Italians do it.

Fedelini is a long round noodle, thicker than angel hair but thinner than spaghetti. You can use any long pasta if fedelini is not available.

SERVES 4 AS A SIDE DISH OR 2 AS AN ENTRÉE

½ pound fedelini noodles
½ cup olive oil
1 sprig fresh rosemary
4 garlic cloves, chopped
1 pound baby zucchini, thinly sliced
2 cups Chicken Broth (page 40) or canned low-sodium chicken broth
1 teaspoon kosher salt
¼ teaspoon black pepper
Shaved Parmesan cheese, for garnish
2 tablespoons chopped fresh basil leaves, for garnish

Bring a large pot of water to a boil over high heat. Add the fedelini and cook until *al dente*. Drain and set aside.

Place a large skillet over medium-high heat and, when it is hot, add the oil. Add the rosemary and garlic and cook until the garlic is lightly toasted, about 3 minutes. Add the zucchini and stir well. Add the Chicken Broth and cook until the zucchini is tender, about 20 minutes. Add the fedelini, salt, and pepper and cook for 1 minute.

Serve immediately, garnished with the shaved Parmesan cheese and chopped basil.

Spaghetti with Hazelnuts and Green Beans

I love this dish: The flavor and texture of the overcooked green beans adds such a rich character to the sauce. Don't be tempted to undercook the beans; they will add nothing. Once you've mastered the technique of overcooking the green beans, you'll add them to many dishes, like boiled potatoes.

You can dress this up by adding 1 pound of cooked shrimp. Toss them in with the hazelnuts.

SERVES 4

1 teaspoon olive oil
1 Spanish onion, chopped
¾ pound green beans, trimmed (about 3 cups)
3 cups water
1 pound spaghetti
2 tablespoons unsalted butter
1 cup chopped hazelnuts
Shaved or grated Parmesan cheese, for garnish

Place a large skillet over medium-high heat and, when it is hot, add the oil. Add the onion and cook until golden, about 5 to 7 minutes. Add the beans, stir to coat, and then add the water. Lower the heat to medium and cook until the beans are tender and the water has evaporated, about 20 to 25 minutes.

While the beans are cooking, prepare the spaghetti and the hazelnuts: Bring a large pot of water to a boil over high heat. Add the spaghetti and cook until *al dente*. Drain and set aside.

Place the butter in a medium-sized skillet over medium heat and cook until browned, about 3 to 4 minutes. Add the hazelnuts and cook until the hazelnuts are browned, about 3 to 4 minutes.

Add the hazelnuts and spaghetti to the beans, stir and cook for 1 minute. Serve immediately, garnished with the Parmesan cheese.

Spaghetti with Brown Butter and Caramelized Onions

*B*rowning the butter and caramelizing the onions create an amazingly sweet and nutty sauce.

This is wonderful on polenta or risotto or served over grilled chicken.

SERVES 4

1 pound spaghetti
½ teaspoon cornstarch
1 tablespoon water
¼ cup unsalted butter
1 garlic clove, sliced
1½ to 2 cups Caramelized Onions (page 31)
1 teaspoon kosher salt
½ teaspoon black pepper
4 to 6 fresh sage leaves, cut in chiffonade, for garnish

Bring a large pot of water to a boil over high heat. Add the spaghetti and cook until *al dente*. Reserving ½ cup pasta water, drain and set aside.

Place the cornstarch and water in a small bowl and mix until well combined. Set aside.

While the spaghetti is cooking, prepare the brown butter: Place the butter and garlic in a medium-sized skillet over medium-high heat and cook until the butter is bubbly and browned, about 2 to 3 minutes. Add the Caramelized Onions and the reserved pasta water and cook for 2 minutes. Add the cornstarch mixture and cook for 1 minute. Transfer to a blender or food processor fitted with a steel blade and process until smooth. Return to the skillet and cook for 1 minute. Add the spaghetti, salt, and pepper.

Serve immediately, garnished with the sage.

Chickpea Fedelini with Shrimp and Tomatoes

he first time Sally made this, she was sure that her children Ben and Lauren (who will eat almost anything) wouldn't eat it. But *au contraire,* they loved it. There is something about the creamy silkiness of the chickpea purée that our kids love. You might not, however, want to tell them that the sauce is made from chickpeas.

You can substitute white beans for the chickpeas, eliminate the shrimp, or substitute chicken or, Lauren's favorite, lobster.

SERVES 4

1 pound fedelini noodles or a chunky pasta such as notelle
2 cups cooked chickpeas, rinsed and drained
1¼ cups Chicken Broth (page 40) or canned low-sodium chicken broth
1 tablespoon olive oil
2 garlic cloves, thinly sliced
1 pound large shrimp, shelled, deveined, and halved lengthwise
4 to 5 plum tomatoes (about ¾ pound), thinly sliced
2 tablespoons chopped fresh parsley leaves
1½ teaspoons kosher salt
1 teaspoon black pepper
4 parsley sprigs, for garnish

Bring a large pot of water to a boil over high heat. Add the fedelini and cook until *al dente.* Drain and set aside.

Place 1½ cups chickpeas and the Chicken Broth in a blender and purée. Set aside.

Place a skillet over medium-high heat and, when it is hot, add the oil. Sprinkle the shrimp with ½ teaspoon each salt and pepper. Add the garlic to the pan and, when it has lightly browned, add the shrimp and sear it on both sides. Set the

shrimp aside. Add the tomatoes, sear them, and then return the shrimp to the skillet. Add the chopped parsley, remaining 1 teaspoon salt, remaining ½ teaspoon pepper, and remaining ½ cup chickpeas.

Transfer the chickpea and Chicken Broth mixture to an additional large skillet and cook over medium heat until heated through, about 2 to 3 minutes. Add the cooked noodles and the reserved chickpea and shrimp mixture.

Divide between 4 shallow bowls and serve immediately, garnished with a parsley sprig.

Chicken and Gorgonzola with Fedelini Noodles

*I*f Roquefort is the aristocrat of blue cheeses then Gorgonzola is the black sheep: raffish, a little too strong for some tastes, yet with certain undeniable charms. In fact, Gorgonzola is the cheese I eat when I'm feeling rowdy. I toss it with gnocchi or polenta or pile it on toast.

SERVES 4

*1 pound boneless, skinless chicken breast, trimmed of excess fat
    and cubed*
1 teaspoon kosher salt
½ teaspoon black pepper
1 tablespoon olive oil
2½ cups Chicken Broth (page 40) or canned low-sodium chicken broth
¾ cup Italian Gorgonzola cheese (see note on page 62)
2 tablespoons unsalted butter
2 tablespoons chopped fresh parsley leaves
¼ cup toasted walnuts (see note on page 67), finely chopped
½ cup finely chopped bread crumbs
1 to 1¼ pounds fedelini noodles or spaghetti

Sprinkle the chicken with ½ teaspoon salt and ¼ teaspoon pepper. Place a large skillet over medium heat and, when it is hot, add the oil. Add the chicken and cook until lightly browned on all sides, about 3 minutes.

Add the Chicken Broth and cook until it is thick and has reduced by two-thirds. Add ¼ cup Gorgonzola cheese and stir until well blended. Add the butter and parsley.

Place the walnuts, bread crumbs, remaining ½ teaspoon salt, and remaining ¼ teaspoon pepper in a bowl and toss to combine.

Bring a large pot of water to a boil over high heat. Add the noodles and cook until *al dente*. Drain, add to the Gorgonzola cheese and chicken mixture, and stir to combine.

Divide between four shallow bowls. Sprinkle with the walnut and bread crumb mixture.

Serve immediately, garnished with the remaining ½ cup shaved Gorgonzola cheese.

POLENTA *and* RISOTTO

Polenta

Polenta can be served soft as soon as it is ready, mashed potato style, or cooled on a plate or baking sheet until firm, cut into squares or triangles, and then pan-fried or grilled.

To pan-fry, place a large skillet over medium-high heat and when it is hot, add a small amount of olive oil. Add the polenta and fry until golden, about 2 minutes per side.

To grill, brush with olive oil and grill until golden, about 2 minutes per side. You can also make croutons with any leftover polenta.

SERVES 6 TO 8

8 cups water
2 teaspoons kosher salt
2 cups stone-ground yellow cornmeal
2 tablespoons unsalted butter
¼ cup light or heavy cream
2 tablespoons freshly grated Parmesan cheese
2 tablespoons freshly grated Romano cheese
½ teaspoon black pepper, or more to taste

Place the water and salt in a medium-sized saucepan and bring to a boil over high heat. Gradually pour in the cornmeal, whisking all the while.

When the mixture begins to bubble, lower the heat to medium-low and cook until the cornmeal begins to thicken, about 10 to 15 minutes.

Slowly whisk in the remaining ingredients. Continue cooking until the polenta just begins to pull away from the sides of the pan.

Serve immediately, pan-fry or grill.

Creamy Cheddar and Spinach Polenta

*I*f your kids don't appreciate spinach, you can eliminate it. You can also substitute half the amount of goat, feta, or Fontina for the cheddar.

Serve with Olivia's Crunchy Chicken (page 191).

SERVES 4

4 cups water

1 teaspoon kosher salt

1 cup stone-ground yellow cornmeal

½ cup milk

1 bunch leaf spinach, well washed and coarsely chopped

1 to 1½ cups shredded sharp cheddar cheese

½ teaspoon black pepper, or more to taste

Place the water and salt in a medium-sized saucepan and bring to a boil over high heat. Gradually pour in the cornmeal, whisking all the while.

When the mixture begins to bubble, lower the heat to medium-low and cook until the cornmeal begins to thicken, about 10 to 15 minutes.

Slowly whisk in the remaining ingredients. Continue cooking until the polenta just begins to pull away from the sides of the pan.

Serve immediately.

Sweet Potato Polenta

*I*n my quest to improve upon the basic, and I think dull, polenta, I combined sweet potatoes with cornmeal to create a uniquely American flavor.

This is good with pork, lamb, and Black Bean Chili (page 98).

SERVES 6

1 large sweet potato, peeled and diced
8 cups water
2 cups stone-ground yellow cornmeal
1 tablespoon maple syrup
½ cup heavy cream
1 teaspoon kosher salt
½ teaspoon black pepper

Place the sweet potato and water in a large pot and bring to a boil over high heat. Cook until very tender, about 20 minutes. Gradually pour in the cornmeal, whisking all the while and pressing down on the potato to break it up, being sure some texture remains.

When the mixture begins to bubble, lower the heat to medium-low and cook until the cornmeal begins to thicken, about 10 to 15 minutes.

Slowly whisk in the remaining ingredients. Continue cooking until the polenta just begins to pull away from the sides of the pan.

Serve immediately.

Chicken Broccoli Risotto

*L*ong and slow is the only way to cook broccoli. None of this *al dente* stuff for me. Be sure to just cover the broccoli with water rather than drown it; you don't want a lot of stinky broccoli water. If you don't like broccoli rabe, this dish could change your mind. But if you're going to be stubborn, make this with an entire head of broccoli.

SERVES 4

1 tablespoon olive oil
1 small Spanish onion, chopped
2 garlic cloves, thinly sliced
½ head broccoli, stems and florets chopped
½ bunch broccoli rabe, trimmed and chopped
8 cups Chicken Broth (page 40) or canned low-sodium chicken broth
1 boneless, skinless chicken breast, trimmed of excess fat and diced
2 cups arborio rice
2 tablespoons unsalted butter, at room temperature (optional)
½ teaspoon kosher salt
½ teaspoon black pepper
½ cup freshly grated Parmesan cheese
⅓ to ½ cup chopped fresh basil leaves, plus additional for garnish

Place a large straight-sided, nonreactive stainless steel, nonstick, or lined copper saucepan over medium-high heat and, when it is hot, add the oil. Add the onion, garlic, broccoli, and broccoli rabe, stirring well after each addition, and cook until toasted, about 5 to 7 minutes. Add enough Chicken Broth to cover and cook until almost all the broth has evaporated, about 12 to 15 minutes. Add the chicken and cook until it turns white, about 2 to 3 minutes. Add the rice and stir until it is well coated. Continue adding Chicken Broth, 1 cup at a time, stirring with each addition, until all the liquid has been absorbed, about 18 to 20 minutes.

Add the butter, if desired, and the salt, pepper, Parmesan cheese, and basil. Serve immediately, garnished with additional basil.

Carrot Risotto with Parsnips and Lentils de Puy

*S*ally asked me to make a risotto without any cheese, and, challenged, I made a carrot risotto. But then Joe Brenner, Olives' sous chef, came in and said it tasted like the kind of thing you threw together when you had nothing in the kitchen except carrots and rice. Wounded, I tinkered away until I had a risotto that thrilled all three of us.

SERVES 6 TO 8

1 tablespoon olive oil
1 Spanish onion, chopped
3 parsnips, peeled, if desired, and diced
2 garlic cloves, finely chopped
Pinch saffron
1 jalapeño pepper, seeds discarded and meat finely diced
¾ cup lentils de Puy (French lentils) (see note)
2 bay leaves
2 cups arborio rice
½ cup white wine
4 to 5 cups Chicken Broth (page 40) or canned low-sodium chicken broth
3 cups fresh carrot juice, juiced at home or store bought
1 teaspoon sherry vinegar
2 tablespoons unsalted butter (optional)
4 scallion greens, chopped, for garnish

Place a large, straight-sided, nonreactive stainless steel, nonstick, or lined copper saucepan over medium-high heat and, when it is hot, add the oil. Add the onion, parsnips, garlic, saffron, jalapeño pepper, lentils, and bay leaves, stirring well after each addition, and cook until the onion is transparent and soft, about 7 to 10 minutes. Lower the heat to low and cook for 10 minutes.

Add the rice and stir well until it is well coated. Add the wine and cook until it is absorbed.

Add the Chicken Broth, 1 cup at a time, stirring with each addition, until all the liquid has been absorbed, about 12 to 15 minutes. Add the carrot juice, 1 cup at a time, stirring with each addition, until all the liquid has been absorbed, about 7 to 10 minutes. Add the vinegar and cook for 2 minutes. Add the butter, if desired.

Divide the risotto among 6 to 8 shallow bowls and serve immediately, garnished with the scallion greens.

NOTE: You can substitute regular lentils *but* . . . the beauty of lentils de Puy is their firm texture. If you use another kind, they will either be undercooked or mushy in comparison.

Four-Onion Risotto

Four-Onion Risotto may sound overpoweringly strong, but something magical happens when you combine so many members of the lily family. The subtle, delicate onion flavor is heightened and yet mellowed by the swirl of goat cheese at the end. Alice Waters made this combination famous on her pizza, but I think it's even better in risotto.

SERVES 6 TO 8

2 tablespoons unsalted butter
2 cups thinly sliced leeks
1 Spanish onion, diced
5 to 6 shallots, thinly sliced
6 garlic cloves, thinly sliced
2 cups arborio rice
½ cup white wine
6 cups Chicken Broth (page 40) or canned low-sodium chicken broth
2 tablespoons fresh thyme leaves
½ cup goat cheese

Place a large, straight-sided, nonreactive stainless steel, nonstick, or lined copper saucepan over medium-high heat and, when it is hot, add the butter. Add the leeks, onion, shallots, and garlic, stirring well after each addition, and cook until they are transparent and soft, about 7 to 10 minutes.

Add the rice and stir until it is well coated. Add the wine and cook until it is absorbed.

Add the Chicken Broth, 1 cup at a time, stirring with each addition, until all the liquid has been absorbed, about 18 to 20 minutes. Add 1 tablespoon thyme and the goat cheese.

Divide the risotto among 6 to 8 shallow bowls and serve immediately, garnished with the remaining 1 tablespoon thyme.

Roasted Fennel and Shrimp Risotto

*L*ike shrimp and garlic, made famous by millions of Scampi dishes, shrimp and fennel, or anise, make a marriage as wonderful but less often seen. Roasting the fennel renders it sweeter, milder, and meatier, so even those who dislike the licorice flavor of raw fennel will find this dish appealing.

SERVES 4

2 to 3 fennel bulbs (should yield about 1 cup fennel meat)
1 tablespoon olive oil
1 teaspoon kosher salt
½ teaspoon black pepper
1 tablespoon unsalted butter
1 cup arborio rice
6 cups Chicken Broth (page 40) or canned low-sodium chicken broth
1 cup heavy cream
½ teaspoon saffron threads
Pinch cayenne
8 large shrimp, peeled, deveined, and cut into thirds
5 tablespoons chopped fresh basil leaves
¼ cup freshly grated Parmesan cheese
4 basil sprigs, for garnish

Preheat the oven to 325 degrees.

Sprinkle the fennel with the oil, ½ teaspoon salt, and the pepper. Place on a baking sheet, transfer to the oven, and bake until almost burnt on the outside, about 1½ hours. Peel off and discard the outer leaves. Split and scoop out the middle. Set aside.

Place a large, straight-sided, nonreactive stainless steel, nonstick, or lined copper saucepan over medium-high heat and, when it is hot, add the butter. Add the fennel and stir. Add the rice and stir until it is well coated. Add the Chicken Broth, 1 cup at a time, stirring with each addition, until all the liquid has been absorbed, about 18 to 20 minutes.

While the risotto is cooking, prepare the saffron shrimp: Place the cream and saffron in a small pan and bring to a boil. Lower the heat to low and cook for 5 minutes. Add the cayenne and shrimp and cook until the shrimp is done, about 4 to 5 minutes. Add the remaining ½ teaspoon salt and 1 tablespoon basil.

When the risotto is done, add the remaining 4 tablespoons basil and the Parmesan cheese. Divide the risotto among 4 shallow bowls and pour equal amounts of the saffron cream and shrimp on top.

Serve immediately, garnished with a basil sprig.

Chive Risotto

*M*ore delicate than their cousin, the onion, chives lend a wonderful freshness and lightness to this bright green risotto. Be sure not to cook the chive oil or the chives.

Use this as an accompaniment to fish, as a first course risotto, or as the main course for a luscious light luncheon.

SERVES 4

2 tablespoons unsalted butter
1 small Spanish onion, minced
1 cup arborio rice
5½ cups Chicken Broth (page 40) or canned low-sodium chicken broth
2 to 3 tablespoons Chive Oil (page 34)
1 teaspoon kosher salt
1 cup freshly grated Parmesan cheese
¼ cup chopped chives, for garnish

Place a large, straight-sided, nonreactive stainless steel, nonstick, or lined copper saucepan over medium-high heat and, when it is hot, add 1 tablespoon butter. Add the onion and cook until it is transparent and soft, about 7 to 10 minutes. Add the rice and stir until it is well coated. Add the Chicken Broth, 1 cup at a time, stirring with each addition, until all the liquid has been absorbed, about 18 to 20 minutes.

Off heat, add the Chive Oil, the remaining 1 tablespoon butter, salt, and Parmesan cheese, stirring well after each addition.

Serve immediately, garnished with the chives.

Roasted Radicchio Risotto

I like radicchio best cooked; the charred crisp edges contrast with the silky rich, sweet texture.

SERVES 4

For the roasted radicchio:

2 garlic cloves, finely chopped
1 tablespoon olive oil
1 teaspoon chopped fresh rosemary leaves
¼ teaspoon kosher salt
Pinch black pepper
1 large head radicchio, well washed and halved through the root

For the risotto:

1 tablespoon unsalted butter
1 Spanish onion, chopped
2 garlic cloves, minced
1 cup arborio rice
6 cups Chicken Broth (page 40) or canned low-sodium chicken broth
¼ teaspoon kosher salt
½ teaspoon black pepper
1 teaspoon chopped fresh rosemary leaves
½ teaspoon Dijon mustard
¼ cup freshly grated Parmesan cheese
¼ cup grated Fontina cheese
4 rosemary sprigs, for garnish

Place the garlic, oil, rosemary, salt, and pepper in a large bowl and mix well. Add the radicchio and gently toss so that it is well coated. Cover and let marinate at room temperature at least 1 hour.

Preheat the oven to 425 degrees.

Place the radicchio in a baking pan and pour the marinade on top. Transfer to the oven and roast until the edges are crisp and just beginning to look burnt, about 20 to 25 minutes. When the radicchio is cool enough to handle, cut it into thin strips.

To make the risotto: Place a large, straight-sided, nonreactive stainless steel, nonstick, or lined copper saucepan over medium-high heat and, when it is hot, add 1 tablespoon butter. Add the onion and garlic and cook until they are transparent and soft, about 7 to 10 minutes. Add the rice and stir until it is well coated. Add the Chicken Broth, 1 cup at a time, stirring with each addition, until all the liquid has been absorbed, about 18 to 20 minutes.

Add the remaining salt and pepper, the roasted radicchio, rosemary, Dijon mustard, and Parmesan and Fontina cheeses.

Divide the risotto among 4 shallow bowls and serve immediately, garnished with a rosemary sprig.

Asparagus Butter Risotto with Shrimp

The first time I had this dish it was made with wild asparagus, which, although not essential, is even more intense in flavor.

Whipping the asparagus into the butter seems to amplify the flavor of the asparagus. The asparagus butter can be served alone on pasta, polenta, or grilled fish. Keep a stick in your freezer.

You can substitute artichoke bottoms or hearts for the asparagus.

SERVES 4

3 tablespoons unsalted butter, at room temperature
¾ pound asparagus, stems peeled, chopped, and blanched, tips set aside
½ cup chopped fresh basil leaves
3 garlic cloves, chopped
1 leek, well washed and chopped
1 cup arborio rice
½ cup white wine
4 to 4½ cups Chicken Broth (page 40) or canned low-sodium
   chicken broth
16 large shrimp, cleaned, deveined and roughly chopped
1 cup freshly grated Parmesan cheese
½ to 1 teaspoon kosher salt
½ teaspoon black pepper
4 rosemary sprigs, for garnish

To make the asparagus butter: Place 2 tablespoons butter, the asparagus stems, and the basil in a food processor fitted with a steel blade and purée. Set aside.

To make the risotto: Place a large, straight-sided, nonreactive stainless steel, nonstick, or lined copper saucepan over medium-high heat and, when it is hot, add the remaining 1 tablespoon butter. Add the garlic and leek and cook until they are transparent and soft, about 7 to 10 minutes. Add the rice and stir until it is well coated.

Add the wine and cook until it has been absorbed. Add 2 cups Chicken Broth, 1 cup at a time, stirring with each addition, until all the liquid has been absorbed, about 10 minutes. Add the asparagus tips, shrimp, and remaining 2 cups Chicken Broth and cook until all the liquid has been absorbed.

Add the asparagus butter, Parmesan cheese, salt, and pepper, stirring well after each addition, and cook for 1 to 2 minutes.

Divide the risotto among 4 shallow bowls and serve immediately, garnished with the rosemary sprigs.

Spring Risotto with Arugula Pesto and Pea Shoots

*L*iving in New England we don't make this risotto until the beginning of June at the earliest, because that's when the so-called spring vegetables start really getting good. We continue to serve it through August. If pea shoots are unavailable, substitute snow peas.

SERVES 8 AS AN APPETIZER OR 4 AS AN ENTRÉE

1 large bunch arugula, well washed
1 cup freshly grated Parmesan cheese, plus additional for garnish
5 tablespoons olive oil
1½ teaspoons kosher salt
1 Spanish onion, finely chopped
2 garlic cloves, finely chopped
2 cups arborio rice
½ cup white wine
7½ to 8 cups Chicken Broth (page 40) or canned low-sodium
    chicken broth
3 tablespoons unsalted butter
4 cups pea shoots
1 cup fresh or frozen peas, blanched if fresh
1 cup fresh fava beans, blanched
1 cup asparagus tips, blanched
½ teaspoon black pepper

To make the arugula pesto: Place the arugula in a food processor fitted with a steel blade and process until chopped. Add the Parmesan cheese, 4 tablespoons oil, and ½ teaspoon salt and process until emulsified. Set aside.

To make the risotto: Place a large, straight-sided, nonreactive stainless steel, nonstick, or lined copper saucepan over a medium heat and, when it is hot, add the remaining 1 tablespoon oil. Add the onion and garlic and cook until golden, about 4 minutes. Add the rice and stir until it is well coated. Deglaze the pan with the wine and cook until it has been absorbed by the rice.

Add the Chicken Broth, 1 cup at a time, stirring with each addition, until all the liquid has been absorbed, about 18 to 20 minutes.

Place a large skillet over medium-high heat and, when it is hot, add 1 tablespoon butter. Add the pea shoots and cook until they are wilted, about 3 minutes. Set aside.

When the risotto is almost ready, stir in the reserved arugula pesto, the peas, fava beans, asparagus tips, remaining 2 tablespoons butter, remaining 1 teaspoon salt, and pepper.

Divide among 4 to 8 shallow bowls and serve immediately, garnished with the reserved pea shoots and the additional Parmesan cheese.

PIZZA

Figs Pizza Dough

With a little bit of time and effort, Figs pizza dough can easily be mastered. However, if you don't have the time or are intimidated by working with yeast, call your local pizza place and see if they'll sell you some of their dough. In some areas you can buy refrigerated dough (*not* the kind in a tube); this would also work well. If you use a heavy, bready, prebaked, vacuum-packed pizza crust, it just won't be the same.

Our dough is far wetter than you'd ever believe; it makes a light, crisp crust. It may take you a few tries before you get it right. Be patient and err on the side of underworking the dough; if you overwork it, the crust will be tough and dry.

This recipe makes four rounds of pizza, though the topping recipes make two pizzas. We figure that this way you only have to make the dough every other time. Simply wrap the remaining two balls of dough in plastic wrap and freeze for up to two weeks.

MAKES FOUR 8- TO 10-INCH PIZZAS
(SERVES 1 TO 2 PEOPLE PER PIZZA)

¼ cup whole-wheat flour
3½ cups all-purpose flour, plus additional for rolling
2 teaspoons (¼ ounce) fresh yeast
2 teaspoons kosher salt
2 teaspoons sugar
2 teaspoons olive oil
1⅔ cups lukewarm water

Place the whole-wheat flour, all-purpose flour, yeast, salt, and sugar in a mixer fitted with a dough hook. While the mixer is running, gradually add the oil and water. Knead on low speed until the dough is firm and smooth, about 10 minutes.

Divide the dough into four balls, about 7½ ounces each. Line two cookie sheets with parchment paper. Place two balls on a sheet and cover with a damp towel. Let them rise in a warm spot until they have doubled in bulk, about 2 hours.

To roll out the dough: Dab your fingers in flour and then place 1 ball on a generously floured work surface and press down in the center with the tips of your fingers, spreading the dough with your hand. When the dough has doubled in width, use a floured rolling pin and roll out until it is very thin, like flatbread. The outer border should be a little thicker than the inner circle. Pick the dough up with a spatula or the back of a knife, allowing it to fold up almost like an umbrella and transfer it to a paddle. Do not worry that the pizza is not round, you are looking for an 8- to 10-inch shape, a cross between an oval and a rectangle. If you get a hole, simply pinch the edges back together. Repeat with the remaining balls and proceed with any of the following recipes.

White Bean Hummus and Asiago Pizza

*F*our years ago, Olivia entered me in a Cooking Light contest to create the "best pizza ever," while meeting healthy (low-fat) guidelines. Off I went to Birmingham, Alabama, for four days. It was not a great time for us financially, what with the ups and downs of the restaurant business, and Olivia figured that if I won the $3,000 prize, she could justify sending Oliver to camp for the summer. Guilt-free.

This is the pizza that won: The creamy elegance of the white bean hummus contrasts nicely with the sharpness of the arugula. It's still one of my favorites. Oliver doesn't eat it, but he had a great summer at camp.

MAKES 2 PIZZAS

2 pizza rounds (page 150)
Cornmeal for sprinkling
2 teaspoons olive oil
½ teaspoon minced garlic
2 pinches kosher salt
2 pinches black pepper
½ cup freshly grated Asiago cheese
½ cup Caramelized Onions (page 31)
2 tablespoons freshly shaved Parmesan cheese
1½ bunches arugula, well washed and dried
3 tablespoons Quick White Bean Hummus (page 68)

One hour prior to cooking, place a baking stone in the oven and preheat it to 500 degrees.

Roll out 1 pizza round as thinly as possible. Place it on a pizza peel sprinkled with cornmeal. Cover the surface with 1 teaspoon oil, ¼ teaspoon minced garlic, and 1 pinch each salt and pepper. Be sure to leave an outer lip of 1 inch all the way around.

Evenly distribute 2 tablespoons Asiago cheese. Top with half the Caramelized Onions and sprinkle with 1 tablespoon Parmesan cheese.

Shake the paddle lightly and slide the pizza onto the baking stone. Bake until browned, about 6 to 7 minutes. Evenly distribute half the arugula and then drizzle 1½ tablespoons Quick White Bean Hummus over the top. Transfer to a firm surface and cut into slices.

Serve immediately.

Repeat with the remaining dough.

Pizza Bianco

*I*f you want to test the true quality of a crust, make a Pizza Bianco. If you are feeling creative, make up you own salad. It's not traditional, but what's really great on top is a Caesar salad.

I wish I could say I invented this, but it has been popular in parts of Italy for years. If you are going to make the salad with arugula, buy the best organic greens you can find; it will have an even more intense peppery quality.

Be careful not to overdo the caramelized onions and be sure you use *all* the oil. The onions need to get between the oil and the cheese, or the pizza will burn easily.

MAKES 2 PIZZAS

2 pizza rounds (page 150)
Cornmeal for sprinkling
2 teaspoons olive oil
½ teaspoon minced garlic
2 pinches kosher salt
2 pinches black pepper
3 cups arugula (2 to 3 bunches), well washed and torn apart
4 plum tomatoes, cut into ¼-inch rounds
2 tablespoons extra-virgin olive oil
2 teaspoons balsamic vinegar
4 teaspoons freshly grated Parmesan cheese
6 slices mozzarella cheese
½ cup Caramelized Onions (page 31)

One hour prior to cooking, place a baking stone in the oven and preheat it to 500 degrees.

Roll out 1 pizza dough as thinly as possible. Place it on a pizza peel sprinkled with cornmeal. Cover the surface with 1 teaspoon olive oil, ¼ teaspoon minced garlic, and 1 pinch each salt and pepper. Be sure to leave an outer lip of 1 inch all the way around.

Place the arugula, tomatoes, extra-virgin olive oil, vinegar, and 2 teaspoons Parmesan cheese in a bowl and toss to combine. Set aside.

Evenly distribute 3 slices of mozzarella cheese on the pizza. It is not necessary to cover the bottom completely. Top with ¼ cup Caramelized Onions and sprinkle with 1 teaspoon Parmesan cheese.

Shake the paddle lightly and slide the pizza onto the baking stone. Bake until browned, about 6 to 7 minutes. Evenly distribute half the reserved arugula salad on the pizza, transfer to a firm surface, and cut into slices.

Serve immediately.

Repeat with the remaining dough.

Pizza Classico

*B*uffeto is one of my favorite pizzerias in Rome. Located near the Piazza Navona, down an alleyway, they serve only a few styles of pizza. This is my interpretation of one of their pies.

MAKES 2 PIZZAS

2 pizza rounds (page 150)
Cornmeal for sprinkling
2 pinches kosher salt
2 pinches black pepper
2 tablespoons Basil Oil (page 33)
4 tablespoons Basic Tomato Sauce (page 105)
2 tablespoons freshly shaved Parmesan cheese

One hour prior to cooking, place a baking stone in the oven and preheat it to 500 degrees.

Roll out 1 pizza dough as thinly as possible. Place it on a pizza peel sprinkled with cornmeal. Cover the surface with 1 pinch each salt and pepper. Place 1 tablespoon Basil Oil and 2 tablespoons Basic Tomato Sauce on the pizza and mix together with a wooden spoon. It will form a thin cover on the bottom. Be sure to leave an outer lip of 1 inch all the way around.

Shake the paddle lightly and slide the pizza onto the baking stone. Bake until browned, about 6 to 7 minutes. Sprinkle with 1 tablespoon Parmesan cheese. Transfer to a firm surface and cut into slices.

Serve immediately.

Repeat with the remaining dough.

Oliver Pizza

*N*amed after my son and helper, Oliver, the Oliver Pizza is our version of the traditional pizza and is the most popular pizza we sell. Oliver still eats one a week to ensure quality, but like most children, he asks that we hold the basil; no green stuff for him.

At Figs you can order an Extra Oliver with double cheese.

MAKES 2 PIZZAS

2 pizza rounds (page 150)
Cornmeal for sprinkling
2 teaspoons olive oil
½ teaspoon minced garlic
2 pinches kosher salt
2 pinches black pepper
½ cup Basic Tomato Sauce (page 105)
6 to 8 thin slices mozzarella cheese
12 whole fresh basil leaves
4 teaspoons freshly grated Parmesan cheese

One hour prior to cooking, place a baking stone in the oven and preheat it to 500 degrees.

Roll out 1 pizza dough as thinly as possible. Place it on a pizza peel sprinkled with cornmeal. Cover the surface with 1 teaspoon oil, ¼ teaspoon minced garlic, and 1 pinch each salt and pepper. Be sure to leave an outer lip of 1 inch all the way around.

Evenly distribute ¼ cup Basic Tomato Sauce on the pizza. It is not necessary to cover the bottom completely. Top with 3 to 4 slices of mozzarella cheese, 6 basil leaves, and sprinkle with 2 teaspoons Parmesan cheese.

Shake the paddle lightly and slide the pizza onto the baking stone. Bake until browned, about 6 to 7 minutes. Transfer to a firm surface and cut into slices.

Serve immediately.

Repeat with the remaining dough.

Isabelle's Pizza

$\mathcal{H}$aving named a pizza after Oliver, I noticed that one of Isabelle's favorite foods was asparagus, although she'd probably deny it now. This pizza has become a classic at Figs. It never ceases to amaze me how well these ingredients work together.

MAKES 2 PIZZAS

2 pizza rounds (page 150)
Cornmeal for sprinkling
2 teaspoons olive oil
½ teaspoon minced garlic
2 pinches kosher salt
2 pinches black pepper
6 very thin slices Virginia baked ham
8 thin asparagus spears, blanched and sliced lengthwise
½ cup Caramelized Onions (page 31)
6 ounces aged provolone or mozzarella cheese, thinly sliced or grated
2 tablespoons freshly grated Parmesan cheese
1 scallion, thinly sliced lengthwise, for garnish

One hour prior to cooking, place a baking stone in the oven and preheat it to 500 degrees.

Roll out 1 pizza dough as thinly as possible. Place it on a pizza peel sprinkled with cornmeal. Cover the surface with 1 teaspoon oil, ¼ teaspoon minced garlic, and 1 pinch each salt and pepper. Be sure to leave an outer lip of 1 inch all the way around.

Evenly distribute 3 slices of ham on the pizza. It is not necessary to cover the bottom completely. Top with the 4 asparagus spears and ¼ cup Caramelized Onions and then cover with 3 ounces provolone or mozzarella cheese. Sprinkle with 1 tablespoon Parmesan cheese.

Shake the paddle lightly and slide the pizza onto the baking stone. Bake until browned, about 6 to 7 minutes. Transfer to a firm surface and cut into slices.

Serve immediately, garnished with half the scallion slices.

Repeat with the remaining dough.

Fig and Prosciutto Pizza

One of my favorites, the Fig Pizza is lush and intense, with the sweetness of the Fig Jam contrasting with the salt of the prosciutto and the tang of the Gorgonzola.

You need to take a little extra care when assembling this pizza. The Gorgonzola must go on in droplets rather than in big clumps, and the prosciutto must be paper thin so that it literally melts onto the warm pizza.

MAKES 2 PIZZAS

2 pizza rounds (page 150)
Cornmeal for sprinkling
2 teaspoons olive oil
½ teaspoon minced garlic
2 pinches kosher salt
2 pinches black pepper
1 teaspoon chopped fresh rosemary leaves
½ cup Fig Jam (page 35)
4 ounces Gorgonzola cheese, crumbled into pea-sized pieces
3 ounces thinly sliced prosciutto
1 scallion, thinly sliced lengthwise, for garnish

One hour prior to cooking, place a baking stone in the oven and preheat it to 500 degrees.

Roll out 1 pizza dough as thinly as possible. Place it on a pizza peel sprinkled with cornmeal. Cover the surface with 1 teaspoon oil, ¼ teaspoon minced garlic, 1 pinch each salt and pepper, and ½ teaspoon chopped rosemary. Be sure to leave an outer lip of 1 inch all the way around.

Evenly dot ¼ cup Fig Jam and 2 ounces Gorgonzola cheese on the pizza. Top with half the prosciutto.

Shake the paddle lightly and slide the pizza onto the baking stone. Bake until browned, about 6 to 7 minutes. Transfer to a firm surface and cut into slices.

Serve immediately, garnished with half the sliced scallion.

Repeat with the remaining dough.

Roasted Red Bliss Potato, Toasted Almond Pesto, and Fontina Cheese Pizza

*I*f you think of some of the great peasant food in the world, like knishes and potato tacos, potatoes on pizza seems like a natural combination despite how odd it sounds. It's perfect before running a marathon.

When you make the Almond Pesto for this, be sure to keep it on the chunky side. It makes a great contrast against the soft potato.

MAKES 2 PIZZAS

2 pizza rounds (page 150)
Cornmeal for sprinkling
2 teaspoons olive oil
½ teaspoon minced garlic
2 pinches kosher salt
2 pinches black pepper
½ cup Almond Pesto (page 67)
4 thin slices (about 4 ounces) Fontina cheese
4 roasted red new potatoes, each sliced into 4 to 5 rounds
2 teaspoons freshly grated Parmesan cheese
2 tablespoons toasted slivered almonds, for garnish (see note on page 67)

One hour prior to cooking, place a baking stone in the oven and preheat it to 500 degrees.

Roll out 1 pizza dough as thinly as possible. Place it on a pizza peel sprinkled with cornmeal. Cover the surface with 1 teaspoon oil, ¼ teaspoon minced garlic, and 1 pinch each salt and pepper. Be sure to leave an outer lip of 1 inch all the way around.

Evenly distribute ¼ cup Almond Pesto on the pizza. Top with 2 slices Fontina cheese and 2 sliced potatoes. Sprinkle with 1 teaspoon Parmesan cheese.

Shake the paddle lightly and slide the pizza onto the baking stone. Bake until browned, about 6 to 7 minutes. Transfer to a firm surface and cut into slices.

Serve immediately, garnished with 1 tablespoon almonds.

Repeat with the remaining dough.

Spicy Spinach Pizza with Marinated Tomatoes and Feta Cheese

I was eating spanekopita (a spinach pie made with flaky filo dough) at my favorite Greek restaurant, Periyali, in New York City when it occurred to me how fabulous the superb composition of flavors would be on pizza. It is.

To cover the pizza, the feta needs to be well broken up, and the spinach needs to be separated by hand.

MAKES 2 PIZZAS

2 pizza rounds (page 150)
Cornmeal for sprinkling
2 teaspoons olive oil
½ teaspoon minced garlic
2 pinches kosher salt
2 pinches black pepper

For the spicy spinach:

1 tablespoon extra-virgin olive oil
4 garlic cloves, thinly sliced
6 cups bunch spinach, well washed and torn apart
⅛ teaspoon kosher salt
⅛ teaspoon black pepper

For the marinated tomatoes:

4 plum tomatoes, sliced and quartered
1 tablespoon fresh oregano leaves

1 tablespoon extra-virgin olive oil
⅛ teaspoon black pepper

2 tablespoons Roasted Red Onions (page 29)
4 tablespoons (2 ounces) feta cheese, crumbled
1 teaspoon freshly grated Parmesan cheese

One hour prior to cooking, place a baking stone in the oven and preheat it to 500 degrees.

To make the spicy spinach: Place a small skillet over medium heat and when it is hot, add 1 tablespoon extra-virgin olive oil. Add the garlic and spinach and cook until the spinach is wilted, about 2 minutes. Sprinkle with the salt and pepper. Set aside.

To marinate the tomatoes: Place the tomatoes, oregano, 1 tablespoon extra-virgin olive oil, and pepper in a small mixing bowl and toss to combine. Set aside.

Roll out 1 pizza dough as thinly as possible. Place it on a pizza peel sprinkled with cornmeal. Cover the surface with 1 teaspoon olive oil, ¼ teaspoon minced garlic, and 1 pinch each salt and pepper. Be sure to leave an outer lip of 1 inch all the way around.

Evenly distribute half the spicy spinach on the pizza. Top with half the marinated tomatoes, 1 tablespoon Roasted Red Onions, 2 tablespoons feta cheese, and ½ teaspoon Parmesan cheese.

Shake the paddle lightly and slide the pizza onto the baking stone. Bake until browned, about 6 to 7 minutes. Transfer to a firm surface and cut into slices.

Serve immediately.

Repeat with the remaining dough.

Kielbasa, Sauerkraut, and Potato Pizza with Dijon Mustard Aioli

Although they snickered at first, this pizza is the management team's favorite. They can't exactly explain why, but I think it's the incredible classic combination of hearty charcuterie flavors.

Kielbasa is a long linked, garlicky, smoked, cooked Polish sausage that is usually made from pork but sometimes beef or veal. It can be found in well-stocked supermarkets and specialty food shops. I recommend Hillshire Farms kielbasa because it's tasty and readily available nationwide.

MAKES 2 PIZZAS

2 pizza rounds (page 150)
Cornmeal for sprinkling
2 teaspoons olive oil
½ teaspoon minced garlic
2 pinches kosher salt
2 pinches black pepper
6 ounces kielbasa, sliced into 16 rounds
½ cup sauerkraut
*4 boiled or roasted red new or Yukon gold potatoes, each sliced into 4 to
     5 rounds*
2 slices (2 ounces) aged provolone cheese
4 teaspoons freshly grated Parmesan cheese
1 scallion, sliced lengthwise, for garnish
Mustard Aioli (page 73), for garnish

One hour prior to cooking, place a baking stone in the oven and preheat it to 500 degrees.

Roll out 1 pizza dough as thinly as possible. Place it on a pizza peel sprinkled with cornmeal. Cover the surface with 1 teaspoon oil, ¼ teaspoon minced garlic, and 1 pinch each salt and pepper. Be sure to leave an outer lip of 1 inch all the way around.

Evenly distribute 8 kielbasa rounds on the pizza. Top with ¼ cup sauerkraut, 2 sliced potatoes, and 1 slice provolone cheese. Sprinkle with 2 teaspoons Parmesan cheese.

Shake the paddle lightly and slide the pizza onto the baking stone. Bake until browned, about 6 to 7 minutes. Transfer to a firm surface and cut into slices.

Serve immediately, garnished with half the scallion and lightly drizzled with Mustard Aioli.

Repeat with the remaining dough.

Portobello Mushrooms, Mushroom Purée, and Fontina Cheese Pizza

This is Sally's favorite. When I took it off the menu, she ordered it anyway. And now that she's convinced me to put it back on, I'm discovering I should never have taken it off.

MAKES 2 PIZZAS

2 pizza rounds (page 150)
Cornmeal for sprinkling
2 teaspoons olive oil
½ teaspoon minced garlic
2 pinches kosher salt
2 pinches black pepper
6 ounces Italian Fontina cheese, thinly sliced
1 cup Portobello, Porcini, and Button Mushroom Purée (page 111)
2 portobello mushroom caps, trimmed and thinly sliced on the bias
2 tablespoons freshly grated Parmesan cheese
2 pinches black pepper, for garnish
Tiny drizzle truffle oil (optional), for garnish

One hour prior to cooking, place a baking stone in the oven and preheat it to 500 degrees.

Roll out 1 pizza dough as thinly as possible. Place it on a pizza peel sprinkled with cornmeal. Cover the surface with 1 teaspoon oil, ¼ teaspoon minced garlic, and 1 pinch each salt and pepper. Be sure to leave an outer lip of 1 inch all the way around.

Evenly distribute 3 ounces Fontina cheese on the pizza. Top with ½ cup Portobello, Porcini, and Button Mushroom Purée and 1 mushroom cap and sprinkle with 1½ teaspoons Parmesan cheese.

Shake the paddle lightly and slide the pizza onto the baking stone. Bake until browned, about 6 to 7 minutes. Transfer to a firm surface and cut into slices.

Serve immediately, garnished with 1½ teaspoons Parmesan cheese and 1 pinch black pepper. Drizzle with truffle oil, if desired.

Repeat with the remaining dough.

Portobello Mushrooms, Mushroom Purée, Tomatoes, and Fontina Cheese Pizza

*T*his is our second most popular pizza, although Sally says it doesn't compare with the version without tomatoes (page 170). If you can't find truffle oil, don't worry, but if you can find it splurge. It's expensive, but a little goes a long way. We use the truffle oil as an aroma rather than a flavor—its heady aroma spreads throughout the whole room.

MAKES 2 PIZZAS

2 pizza rounds (page 150)
Cornmeal for sprinkling
2 teaspoons olive oil
½ teaspoon minced garlic
2 pinches kosher salt
2 pinches black pepper
½ cup Roasted Tomato Sauce (page 107)
6 slices (6 ounces) Italian Fontina cheese
½ cup Portobello, Porcini, and Button Mushroom Purée (page 111)
2 portobello mushroom caps, trimmed and thinly sliced and roasted
½ cup Roasted Red Onions (page 29)
2 teaspoons freshly grated Parmesan cheese
1 teaspoon truffle oil
2 teaspoons chopped fresh parsley leaves

One hour prior to cooking, place a baking stone in the oven and preheat it to 500 degrees.

Roll out 1 pizza dough as thinly as possible. Place it on a pizza peel sprinkled with cornmeal. Cover the surface with 1 teaspoon oil, ¼ teaspoon minced garlic, and

1 pinch each salt and pepper. Be sure to leave an outer lip of 1 inch all the way around.

Evenly distribute ¼ cup Roasted Tomato Sauce and 3 slices Fontina cheese on the pizza. Dot with ¼ cup Portobello, Porcini, and Button Mushroom Purée, top with 1 portobello mushroom and half the Roasted Red Onions. Sprinkle with 1 teaspoon Parmesan cheese.

Shake the paddle lightly and slide the pizza onto the baking stone. Bake until browned, about 6 to 7 minutes. Drizzle with ½ teaspoon truffle oil and sprinkle with 1 teaspoon parsley. Transfer to a firm surface and cut into slices.

Serve immediately.

Repeat with the remaining dough.

Clam Pizza

*P*epe's clam pizza is legendary. It was made famous by Pepe's, in New Haven, Connecticut, a world-famous pizzeria whose owner claims to have invented American Pizza. When I was in high school, we used to hang out at Pepe's, but now that I live in Boston, I always stop off on my way to and from New York City, which is less often than I would like.

When you put the clams on the pizza, be sure to include the liquor, which contributes enormous flavor. And don't be tempted to increase the Parmesan cheese; if you do, you'll overwhelm the clams.

Keep the clams refrigerated until ready to use, and shuck quickly.

MAKES 2 PIZZAS

2 pizza rounds (page 150)
Cornmeal for sprinkling
½ teaspoon minced garlic
2 pinches kosher salt
2 pinches black pepper
18 to 24 littleneck clams, well washed, shucked, and very roughly
*   chopped, including the clam liquor*
2 tablespoons extra-virgin olive oil
4 teaspoons fresh oregano leaves
3 tablespoons freshly grated Parmesan cheese
2 tablespoons chopped fresh parsley leaves, for garnish

One hour prior to cooking, place a baking stone in the oven and preheat it to 500 degrees.

At the same time, place the clams and their liquor, the oil, and 1 teaspoon oregano in a bowl; toss to combine and set aside.

Roll out 1 pizza dough as thinly as possible. Place it on a pizza peel sprinkled with cornmeal. Cover the surface with ¼ teaspoon minced garlic, and 1 pinch each salt and pepper. Be sure to leave an outer lip of 1 inch all the way around.

Evenly distribute half the clam mixture, including the liquid, over the pizza. Top with 1 teaspoon oregano and sprinkle with 1 tablespoon Parmesan cheese.

Shake the paddle lightly and slide the pizza onto the baking stone. Bake until browned, about 6 to 7 minutes. Transfer to a firm surface and cut into slices.

Serve immediately, garnished with ½ teaspoon oregano, 1½ teaspoons Parmesan cheese, and 1 tablespoon parsley.

Repeat with the remaining dough.

Fresh Asparagus and Mushroom Purée Pizza

The woodsy flavor of this pizza is the essence of spring. It is one of the most popular pizzas we sell.

MAKES 2 PIZZAS

2 pizza rounds (page 150)
Cornmeal for sprinkling
2 teaspoons olive oil
½ teaspoon minced garlic
2 pinches kosher salt
2 pinches black pepper
6 ounces Italian Fontina cheese, thinly sliced
1 cup Portobello, Porcini, and Button Mushroom Purée (page 111)
12 asparagus spears, peeled and halved lengthwise
2 teaspoons freshly grated Parmesan cheese

One hour prior to cooking, place a baking stone in the oven and preheat it to 500 degrees.

Roll out 1 pizza dough as thinly as possible. Place it on a pizza peel sprinkled with cornmeal. Cover the surface with 1 teaspoon oil, ¼ teaspoon minced garlic, and 1 pinch each salt and pepper. Be sure to leave an outer lip of 1 inch all the way around.

Evenly distribute 3 ounces Fontina cheese on the pizza. Top with ½ cup Portobello, Porcini, and Button Mushroom Purée and 6 asparagus spears and sprinkle with ½ teaspoon Parmesan cheese.

Shake the paddle lightly and slide the pizza onto the baking stone. Bake until browned, about 6 to 7 minutes. Transfer to a firm surface and cut into slices.

Serve immediately, garnished with ½ teaspoon Parmesan cheese.

Repeat with the remaining dough.

Fresh Margherita Pizza

*I*t has been said, the simplest things are the most difficult to do well.

When assembling this pizza, be very careful that no basil oil gets on your peel; it's a horror to get off.

MAKES 2 PIZZAS

2 pizza rounds (page 150)
Cornmeal for sprinkling
½ teaspoon minced garlic
2 pinches kosher salt
2 pinches black pepper
¼ cup Basil Oil (page 33)
6 ounces fresh mozzarella cheese, thinly sliced
2 yellow tomatoes, sliced
2 tablespoons freshly grated Parmesan cheese
2 tablespoons chopped fresh basil or parsley leaves, for garnish

One hour prior to cooking, place a baking stone in the oven and preheat it to 500 degrees.

Roll out 1 pizza dough as thinly as possible. Place it on a pizza peel sprinkled with cornmeal. Cover the surface with ¼ teaspoon minced garlic and 1 pinch each salt and pepper. Be sure to leave an outer lip of 1 inch all the way around.

Evenly distribute 2 tablespoons Basil Oil on the pizza. Top with 3 ounces mozzarella cheese and 1 tomato and sprinkle with 1½ teaspoons Parmesan cheese.

Shake the paddle lightly and slide the pizza onto the baking stone. Bake until browned, about 6 to 7 minutes. Transfer to a firm surface and cut into slices.

Serve immediately, garnished with 1½ teaspoons Parmesan cheese and 1 tablespoon basil or parsley.

Repeat with the remaining dough.

Spicy Shrimp Pizza with Caramelized Leeks and Tomato Sauce

*T*his is one of the more complex pizzas we make, but it is well worth the effort.

MAKES 2 PIZZAS

> *2 pizza rounds (page 150)*
> *Cornmeal for sprinkling*
> *2 teaspoons olive oil*
> *½ teaspoon minced garlic*
> *2 pinches kosher salt*
> *2 pinches black pepper*
> *1 hot pepper (jalapeño, serrano, or cherry), seeded and finely minced, or*
> *1 teaspoon red pepper flakes, finely minced*
> *10 large shrimp, shelled, deveined, and sliced lengthwise*
> *1 cup Basic Tomato Sauce (page 105) or Roasted Tomato Sauce*
> *(page 107)*
> *½ cup Caramelized Leeks (page 31)*
> *6 scallions, sliced lengthwise, for garnish*

One hour prior to cooking, place a baking stone in the oven and preheat it to 500 degrees.

Roll out 1 pizza dough as thinly as possible. Place it on a pizza peel sprinkled with cornmeal. Cover the surface with 1 teaspoon oil, ¼ teaspoon minced garlic, and 1 pinch each salt and pepper. Be sure to leave an outer lip of 1 inch all the way around.

Place the hot pepper and shrimp in a small bowl and mix well, being sure the pepper coats the shrimp.

Evenly distribute ½ cup Basic Tomato Sauce on the pizza. It is not necessary to cover the bottom completely. Top with ¼ cup Caramelized Leeks and half the shrimp.

Shake the paddle lightly and slide the pizza onto the baking stone. Bake until browned, about 6 to 7 minutes. Transfer to a firm surface and cut into slices.

Serve immediately, garnished with half the scallion slices.

Repeat with the remaining dough.

AUTOSTRADA PANINI, BURGERS, *and* OLIVIA'S CRUNCHY CHICKEN

Yellow and Red Tomato, Fresh Mozzarella, and Caramelized Onion Panini

After many trips to Italy, it occurred to me that some of my greatest food memories were stopping at Autostrada, eating panini, the pressed sandwiches so prevalent in Italy. What amazing sandwiches they are: full of flavor, yet light! Although typically we eat a lavish lunch and dinner and everything in between, somehow these always hit the spot.

At Figs, instead of flattening them in a special sandwich press, we top them with a cast-iron pan to weigh them down.

As with our pizzas, exercise restraint; if you overdo it, the filling will squish out the sides.

MAKES 2 PANINI; SERVES 4 FOR LUNCH WITH SOUP

2 pizza rounds (page 150)
1 teaspoon olive oil
Kosher salt
Black pepper
4 thin slices yellow tomato
4 thin slices red tomato
4 thin slices mozzarella cheese
½ cup Caramelized Onions (page 31)

One hour prior to cooking, place a baking stone in the oven and preheat it to 500 degrees.

Roll out 1 pizza dough as thinly as possible. Place it on the stone and cook until lightly browned but not crisp, still soft and pliable, about 2 minutes per side. It should look like pita bread.

Transfer to a work surface and cover half of 1 side with ½ teaspoon oil and 1 pinch each salt and pepper.

Evenly distribute half the tomato slices. Top with 2 slices mozzarella cheese and then half the Caramelized Onions. Sprinkle with salt and pepper. Fold the dough over and place the panini on the stone. Top with either a brick wrapped in foil or a cast-iron skillet and cook for about 2 minutes per side.

Serve immediately.

Repeat with the remaining dough.

These can be assembled ahead of time and baked just before serving.

Inside-Out Bianco Panini

*T*his sandwich has the same combination of flavors as our Pizza Bianco (page 155).

MAKES 2 PANINI; SERVES 4 FOR LUNCH WITH SOUP

For the salad:

1 tomato, diced
2 bunches arugula, well washed and torn apart
1 tablespoon extra-virgin olive oil
2 teaspoons balsamic vinegar
½ teaspoon kosher salt
¼ teaspoon black pepper

For the panini:

2 pizza rounds (page 150)
1 teaspoon olive oil
Kosher salt
Black pepper
½ cup Caramelized Onions (page 31)
¼ cup finely grated Parmesan cheese
4 slices fresh mozzarella cheese

One hour prior to cooking, place a baking stone in the oven and preheat it to 500 degrees.

Place the tomatoes, arugula, extra-virgin olive oil, vinegar, salt, and pepper in a bowl and toss to combine. Set aside.

Roll out 1 pizza dough as thinly as possible. Place it on the stone and cook until lightly browned but not crisp, still soft and pliable, about 2 minutes per side. It should look like pita bread.

Transfer to a work surface and cover half of 1 side with ½ teaspoon olive oil and 1 pinch each salt and pepper.

Evenly distribute ¼ cup Caramelized Onions. Sprinkle half the Parmesan cheese and top with 2 slices mozzarella cheese. Sprinkle with salt and pepper. Fold the dough over and place the panini on the stone. Top with either a brick wrapped in foil or a cast-iron skillet and cook for about 2 minutes per side.

Serve immediately, garnished with half the tomato salad.

Repeat with the remaining dough.

These can be assembled ahead of time and baked just before serving.

Black Olive,
Herbed Goat Cheese,
and Basil Oil Panini

This one's a cinch to make if you have a restaurant staff making all the fixin's. Just kidding. Serve with a fresh beefsteak tomato salad.

You can make your own olive paste, or use a commercial brand like San Remo.

MAKES 2 PANINI; SERVES 4 FOR LUNCH WITH SOUP

2 pizza rounds (page 150)
1 teaspoon olive oil
Kosher salt
Black pepper
2 tablespoons black olive paste
4 tablespoons Herbed Goat Cheese (page 64)
1 tablespoon Basil Oil (page 33)

One hour prior to cooking, place a baking stone in the oven and preheat it to 500 degrees.

Roll out 1 pizza dough as thinly as possible. Place it on the stone and cook until lightly browned but not crisp, still soft and pliable, about 2 minutes per side. It should look like pita bread.

Transfer to a work surface and cover half of 1 side with ½ teaspoon oil and 1 pinch each salt and pepper.

Evenly distribute 1 tablespoon olive paste. Top with 2 tablespoons Herbed Goat Cheese and then drizzle lightly with 1½ teaspoons of Basil Oil. Sprinkle with salt and pepper. Fold the dough over and place the panini on the stone. Top with either a brick wrapped in foil or a cast-iron skillet and cook for about 2 minutes per side.

Serve immediately

Repeat with the remaining dough.

These can be assembled ahead of time and baked just before serving.

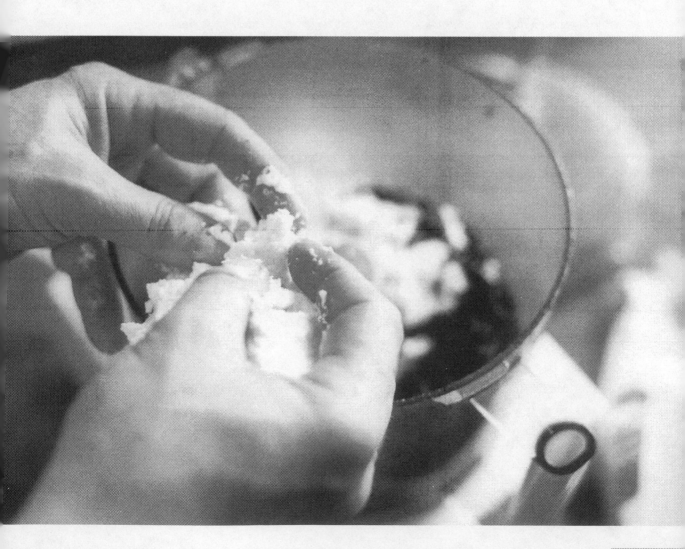

Ham and Mozzarella Panini

*A*n exalted ham and cheese sandwich.

MAKES 2 PANINI; SERVES 4 FOR LUNCH WITH SOUP

2 pizza rounds (page 150)
1 teaspoon olive oil
4 tablespoons Basic Tomato Sauce (page 105) or Roasted Tomato Sauce
    (page 107)
4 tablespoons chopped Virginia baked ham
4 thin slices fresh mozzarella cheese

One hour prior to cooking, place a baking stone in the oven and preheat it to 500 degrees.

Roll out 1 pizza dough as thinly as possible. Place it on the stone and cook until lightly browned but not crisp, still soft and pliable, about 2 minutes per side. It should look like pita bread.

Transfer to a work surface and cover half of 1 side with ½ teaspoon oil and 1 pinch each salt and pepper.

Evenly distribute 2 tablespoons Basic Tomato Sauce or Roasted Tomato Sauce. Top with 2 tablespoons chopped ham and 2 slices mozzarella cheese. Sprinkle with salt and pepper. Fold the dough over and place the panini on the stone. Top with either a brick wrapped in foil or a cast-iron skillet and cook about 2 minutes per side.

Serve immediately

Repeat with the remaining dough.

These can be assembled ahead of time and baked just before serving.

Salmon and Caramelized Onion Panini

*S*erve this for an elegant light lunch or late supper with a simple green salad and a glass of chilled, crisp white wine.

MAKES 2 PANINI

2 pizza rounds (page 150)
1 teaspoon olive oil
Kosher salt
Black pepper
4 tablespoons Caramelized Onions (page 31)
4 tablespoons poached fresh salmon
3 tablespoons mascarpone cheese
2 teaspoons horseradish

One hour prior to cooking, place a baking stone in the oven and preheat it to 500 degrees.

Roll out 1 pizza dough as thinly as possible. Place it on the stone and cook until lightly browned but not crisp, still soft and pliable, about 2 minutes per side. It should look like pita bread.

Transfer to a work surface and cover half of 1 side with ½ teaspoon oil and 1 pinch each salt and pepper.

Evenly distribute 2 tablespoons Caramelized Onions. Top with 2 tablespoons salmon and 1½ tablespoons mascarpone cheese. Sprinkle 1 teaspoon horseradish, salt, and pepper. Fold the dough over and place the panini on the stone. Top with either a brick wrapped in foil or a cast-iron skillet and cook for about 2 minutes per side.

Serve immediately

Repeat with the remaining dough.

These can be assembled ahead of time and baked just before serving.

Chickpea Burger

*Y*ou won't miss the meat in this substantial "burger." It's delicious served with Tomato, Avocado, and Onion Salsa (page 66) or Cucumber Salad (page 51).

MAKES 6 BURGERS

3 cups cooked chickpeas, rinsed and drained

3 tablespoons tahini

1 tablespoon rosemary leaves, coarsely chopped

3 large eggs

2 scallions, chopped

2 tablespoons chopped fresh cilantro leaves

½ Spanish onion, chopped

1½ cups toasted bread crumbs

1 tablespoon olive oil

Place the chickpeas, tahini, rosemary, eggs, and scallions in a food processor fitted with a steel blade and process until completely mixed. Transfer to a large mixing bowl and add the cilantro, onion, and bread crumbs. Form into 6 patties.

Place a large skillet over medium-high heat and, when it is hot, add the oil. Add the patties, 1 at a time, allowing about 30 seconds between additions, and cook until they are well browned, about 4 to 5 minutes on each side.

Serve immediately on a toasted bun or tucked into a small, warmed pita bread.

Olivia's Crunchy Chicken

*T*his recipe is my wife's, and if she made it every single night, our children wouldn't complain.

SERVES 4

4 to 6 chicken breast halves, excess fat removed, meat pounded to an
   even thickness
1 tablespoon Dijon mustard
2 teaspoons minced garlic
⅓ to ½ cup all-purpose flour
1 teaspoon kosher salt
½ teaspoon black pepper
2 large eggs
1 cup bread crumbs
2 tablespoons olive oil
Lemon wedges, for garnish

Place the chicken, mustard, and garlic in a large mixing bowl; cover and refrigerate for 30 minutes. Remove the chicken from the bowl and pat dry with paper towels. (This is a very important step, or the coating will not stick to the chicken.)

Place the flour, salt, and pepper on a large plate. Place the eggs in a shallow bowl and the bread crumbs on another large plate.

Dredge the chicken in the flour mixture, then in the eggs, and then in the bread crumbs.

Place a large nonstick skillet over medium-high heat and, when it is hot, add the oil. Add the chicken breasts and cook until crispy and golden brown, about 5 minutes per side.

Serve immediately with lots of lemon wedges.

Portobello Burger

One of my favorite ways to eat food is breaded: homey, crisp on the outside, creamy on the inside. When you make this, it's hard to believe you're eating a mushroom. You can also substitute these for some of the eggplant in your favorite recipe for Eggplant Parmesan.

SERVES 4

4 large or 8 small portobello mushrooms, stemmed
⅓ to ½ cup all-purpose flour
1 teaspoon kosher salt
½ teaspoon black pepper
2 large eggs
1 cup bread crumbs
2 tablespoons olive oil
4 kaiser or other large rolls
1 red onion, thinly sliced
1 to 2 vine-ripe tomatoes, sliced
4 leaves Boston or Bibb lettuce
Basil Aioli (page 74)

Preheat the oven to 350 degrees.

Place the mushrooms on a baking sheet and transfer to the oven. Cook until browned and tender, about 20 minutes. Set aside to cool.

Place the flour, salt, and pepper on a large plate. Place the eggs in a shallow bowl and the bread crumbs on another large plate. Dredge the mushrooms in the flour mixture, then in the eggs, and then in the bread crumbs.

Place a large nonstick skillet over medium-high heat and, when it is hot, add the oil. Add the mushrooms and cook until crispy and golden brown, about 2 to 3 minutes per side.

Serve immediately on a kaiser roll with the red onion, tomato, lettuce, and Basil Aioli.

DESSERTS

Cranberry Pecan Biscotti

*A*lthough these are incredibly easy and convenient to make (you can do the first baking several days ahead of time), they are equally easy to ruin. The line between crunchy and hard is a fine one, and the truth is that it will take practice and an understanding of your own oven to discover what that line is for you. When in doubt, slightly underbake these cookies, or if you've overbaked them and rendered them hard as a rock, dunk them in coffee or crumble them over ice cream.

Dried apricots, currants, or figs work equally well in this recipe.

MAKES ABOUT 40 TO 48 BISCOTTI

½ cup unsalted butter, cold
¾ cup sugar
¾ cup light brown sugar
2 large eggs, lightly beaten
1½ tablespoons vanilla extract
3 cups all-purpose flour, plus additional for flouring
1½ teaspoons baking powder
¼ teaspoon kosher salt
1 teaspoon ground cardamom
¾ teaspoon ground nutmeg
1 tablespoon freshly grated orange zest (about 1 medium orange)
1 cup dried cranberries
1½ cups pecans, coarsely chopped

Preheat the oven to 350 degrees. Line a baking sheet with parchment or wax paper.

Place the butter and sugars in a large bowl and blend until light. Add the eggs and vanilla and blend until thoroughly combined.

Add the flour, baking powder, salt, cardamom, nutmeg, and orange rind and stir to combine. Add the cranberries and pecans and stir.

Transfer to a floured work surface and knead until the dough just comes together. If necessary, add more flour to the work surface. Divide the dough into 2 halves and shape each into a 12-inch loaf.

Place 1 loaf on the prepared baking sheet and bake until it starts to crack and is a uniform light brown, about 35 minutes. Set aside to cool. Repeat with the remaining loaf.

Lower the temperature to 300 degrees.

Place the loaves on a cutting board and, using a serrated knife, cut each on the diagonal, into 20 to 24 slices, ½-inch thick or for a more delicate biscotti, ¼-inch thick. Place on the baking sheet and bake until lightly toasted, about 10 to 12 minutes. Turn over and bake until dry and crisp, about 5 minutes.

When cooled, store in an airtight container up to 10 to 12 days.

Cardamom Almond Biscotti

*N*o wonder I love cardamom: I recently discovered that it's a member of the ginger family.

Although this spice is more typically seen in Indian, Asian, and Middle Eastern cooking, its peppery warm taste combines well with the almond flavor.

MAKES ABOUT 40 TO 48 BISCOTTI

½ cup unsalted butter, cold

1¾ cups sugar

¼ cup light brown sugar

2 large eggs

1¼ teaspoons vanilla extract

3 cups all-purpose flour

1½ teaspoons baking powder

¼ teaspoon kosher salt

2 tablespoons instant espresso powder

1 teaspoon ground cardamom

1 tablespoon freshly grated orange zest (about 1 medium orange)

¾ cup semisweet chocolate, chopped (optional)

1 cup raw almonds, coarsely chopped

2 teaspoons ground cinnamon

Preheat the oven to 350 degrees. Line a baking sheet with parchment or wax paper.

Place the butter, 1½ cups sugar, and brown sugar in a large bowl and blend until light. Add the eggs, 1 at a time, and the vanilla and blend until thoroughly combined.

Add the flour, baking powder, salt, espresso powder, cardamom, and orange zest and stir to combine. Add the chocolate, if desired, and almonds and stir.

Transfer to a floured work surface and knead until the dough just comes together. If necessary, add more flour to the work surface. Divide the dough into 2 halves and shape each into a 12-inch loaf.

Place 1 loaf on the prepared baking sheet and bake until it starts to crack and is a uniform light brown, about 35 minutes. Set aside to cool. Repeat with the remaining loaf.

Lower the temperature to 300 degrees.

Place the loaves on a cutting board and, using a serrated knife, cut each on the diagonal, into 20 to 24 slices, ½-inch thick.

Place the biscotti on the baking sheet. Place the remaining ¼ cup white sugar and the cinnamon in a small bowl, sprinkle half over the biscotti, and bake until lightly toasted, about 7 to 8 minutes. Turn over, sprinkle the remaining half of the cinnamon sugar over them, and bake until dry and crisp, about 5 minutes.

When cooled, store in an airtight container up tp 10 to 12 days.

Chocolate Hazelnut Biscotti

*T*he combination of chocolate and hazelnuts is both legendary and classic. One taste of these biscotti will tell you why.

MAKES 40 TO 48 BISCOTTI

1¾ cups all-purpose flour
1 cup sugar
⅓ cup cocoa powder
1 tablespoon ground cinnamon
1 teaspoon freshly grated nutmeg
½ teaspoon ground cloves
1 teaspoon baking soda
½ teaspoon kosher salt
½ cup coarsely chopped unsweetened chocolate
½ cup coarsely chopped semisweet chocolate
1¼ cups hazelnuts, coarsely chopped
¼ cup dark roast coffee beans, coarsely chopped (optional)
3 large eggs
1 teaspoon vanilla extract
1 teaspoon Frangelico
2 teaspoons brewed coffee

Preheat the oven to 350 degrees. Line a baking sheet with parchment or wax paper.

Place the flour, sugar, cocoa powder, cinnamon, nutmeg, cloves, baking soda, and salt in a medium bowl and stir to combine. Add the chocolates, hazelnuts, and coffee beans, if desired, and stir.

Place the eggs, vanilla, Frangelico, and coffee in a large bowl; lightly beat and then pour into the flour mixture. Stir until thoroughly combined.

Transfer to a floured work surface and knead until the dough just comes together. It should be stiff. If necessary, add 1 to 2 teaspoons water. If necessary, add more flour to the work surface. Divide the dough into 2 halves and shape each into a 12-inch loaf.

Place 1 loaf on the prepared baking sheet and bake until it starts to crack, about 35 minutes. Set aside to cool. Repeat with the remaining loaf.

Lower the temperature to 300 degrees.

Place the loaves on a cutting board and, using a serrated knife, cut each on the diagonal, into 20 to 24 slices, ½-inch thick.

Place on the baking sheet, transfer to the oven, and bake until lightly toasted, about 7 to 8 minutes. Turn over and bake until dry and crisp, about 5 minutes.

When cooled, store in an airtight container up to 10 to 12 days.

Gingersnaps

*A*hh. I love gingersnaps. I've added fresh ginger to ensure that ginger zing. Serve these with vanilla ice cream and Caramel Sauce (page 225) so that you can really savor them. Or crumble them up to make a cheesecake crust or to toss over ice cream.

Although these are, like most cookies, irresistible right out of the oven, if you want snap and intensity, let them sit at least overnight.

MAKES ABOUT FORTY-EIGHT 2-INCH COOKIES

1 to 2 tablespoons peeled and finely grated fresh gingerroot
½ cup sugar
½ pound unsalted butter, at room temperature
½ cup light brown sugar, lightly packed
½ cup molasses
1 teaspoon kosher salt
2 teaspoons ground cinnamon
1 teaspoon ground cloves
2½ teaspoons ground ginger
3½ cups all-purpose flour
2 teaspoons baking soda

Place the fresh gingerroot and white sugar in a food processor fitted with a steel blade. Pulse until it has a mashlike consistency. Remove and set aside.

Place the butter and brown sugar in the food processor or mixer fitted with a paddle and blend until creamy. Add the ginger mash and blend well.

Add the molasses, salt, cinnamon, cloves, and ground ginger to the food processor and mix well. Add the flour and baking soda and mix until well combined. Cover and refrigerate at least 1 hour.

Form the dough into 2 round logs, about 14 inches long, cover with plastic wrap, and place in the freezer or refrigerator at least 1 hour. When you are ready to

bake them, slice them very thinly and place them on an ungreased cookie sheet. They will not spread.

Preheat the oven to 350 degrees.

Place the sheet in the oven and bake until the edges just begin to darken, about 12 minutes. Remove the baking sheet from the oven and let stand for 1 to 2 minutes. Using a wide spatula, transfer the cookies to wire racks and let cool completely. Let the cookie sheet cool between batches.

When cooled, store in an airtight container up to 5 to 6 days.

Chocolate Chip Cookies

*T*he Toll House Cookie was just made the official cookie of the Commonwealth of Massachusetts. Never one to leave well enough alone, I've added a few new twists to this old classic.

MAKES FORTY-EIGHT 2-INCH COOKIES

2½ sticks (20 tablespoons) unsalted butter, at room temperature
½ cup sugar
1 cup light brown sugar
1 large egg
1 large egg yolk
1 teaspoon vanilla extract
2 teaspoons espresso powder (optional)
1 tablespoon hot water
1 cup rolled oats, pulverized in blender until fine
2 cups all-purpose flour
1 teaspoon baking powder
1 teaspoon baking soda
1 teaspoon kosher salt
3 cups any combination: white, semisweet, or milk chocolate chunks
1 cup toasted walnuts or pecans (optional) (see note on page 67)

Preheat the oven to 325 degrees.

Cream the butter and sugars just until the large lumps disappear. Add the egg, egg yolk, and vanilla and mix until just incorporated, being careful not to over-beat.

Dissolve the espresso powder, if desired, in the hot water in a small glass and add to the butter mixture.

Add the oats, flour, baking powder, baking soda, and salt and mix well, being sure to stir from the bottom. Stir in the chips and, if desired, the nuts.

Drop large tablespoons of dough onto an ungreased cookie sheet. Bake until the cookies are brown on the edges but still soft in the middle, about 12 minutes. Cool the cookie sheet between batches.

When cooled, store in an airtight container up to 5 to 6 days.

White-Chocolate
Challah Pudding

*W*hite-Chocolate Challah Pudding is one of our most popular desserts. This is no run-of-the-mill bread pudding: luscious, smooth, and sensual, it's like sex on a spoon. We see people acting like Meg Ryan in the movie *When Harry Met Sally*, and it's not uncommon for others to tell the waitstaff: "I'll have whatever she's having."

If you only try one recipe in this book, I would recommend that it be this one. Especially on Valentine's Day. Even if you don't like white chocolate (and actually I'm not a big fan), you'll love this. It has the appearance of being light, but in fact it is one of the richest desserts we make. Serve it with a Raspberry Sauce (page 224) to cut the richness or Caramel Sauce (page 225) or chocolate sauce to enhance it.

MAKES 6 SERVINGS

7 large egg yolks
2 whole eggs
2 teaspoons vanilla extract
3 cups heavy cream
1 cup milk
½ cup sugar
10 ounces white chocolate, about 2 cups chopped
4 cups challah cubes, about 1 loaf, crusts removed, if desired

Preheat the oven to 350 degrees.

Place the egg yolks, eggs, and vanilla extract in a small bowl and mix to combine. Set aside.

Place the cream, milk, and sugar in a 2-quart saucepan over medium-high heat and cook until scalded, or when bubbles begin to form around the edges and it has not quite come to a boil, about 7 minutes. Add the white chocolate and mix until fully melted. Gradually add the egg mixture in a slow steady stream, whisking all the while.

Place the bread cubes in an 8 x 8-inch pan and cover with the egg-cream mixture. Press the cubes down and let rest for 15 minutes.

Cover with aluminum foil and place in a larger pan filled halfway with very hot water. Transfer to the oven and bake until firm and, when touched in the middle, the custard does not show up on your finger, about 1 hour and 15 minutes. Check to see if you need to replenish the water after 30 minutes. If so, add enough to keep the water level at the halfway point. Serve warm with fresh berries, Raspberry Sauce, or Caramel Sauce.

Torta Caprese

I don't typically like very sweet desserts, but this one is like a nutty, elegant, slightly undercooked brownie. It's great for breakfast.

Later in the day, you might try it with coffee ice cream or Amaretto spiked whipped cream and a few additional almonds for garnish.

You can substitute an equal amount of hazelnuts or walnuts for the almonds.

SERVES 8

½ pound bittersweet chocolate, chopped
½ pound toasted, sliced almonds (about 1½ cups) (see note on page 67)
1 heaping cup sugar
6 large eggs, at room temperature and separated
½ teaspoon vanilla extract
⅛ teaspoon cream of tartar

Preheat the oven to 325 degrees. Line a 9-inch round pan with parchment or wax paper.

Place the chocolate, almonds, and sugar in a food processor fitted with a steel blade and process until grainy. Transfer to a large mixing bowl.

Place the egg yolks and vanilla in the bowl of a mixer fitted with a whisk attachment and whip until the mixture turns light yellow and forms a ribbon. Fold into the chocolate mixture, stirring well until the chocolate is incorporated.

Place the egg whites and cream of tartar in the bowl of a mixer fitted with a whisk attachment and whip until they hold stiff peaks. Fold into the chocolate mixture.

Transfer to the prepared pan. Place in the oven and bake until the top is light brown, about 1 hour.

Cool slightly and serve.

Vanilla Pound Cake

*I*f there's any cake that brings me back to my childhood, it's pound cake. I love it: we used to eat it in the morning toasted and buttered.

The undetectable taste of the white chocolate gives this rendition a more intense vanilla flavor. I still like it toasted, with a crispy outside and tender dense inside.

Legally called white confectionery coating, white chocolate is technically not chocolate at all because, although it is made from cocoa butter, there is no chocolate or cocoa in it.

Although it's great as is, at Figs, we rarely serve this without one of the following: candied lemon or grapefruit rind; whipped cream flavored with Grand Marnier, Framboise, or Calvados; Caramel Sauce (page 225); Mango Caramel Sauce (page 225); or Raspberry Sauce (page 224).

SERVES 8 TO 10

4 ounces white chocolate, chopped
3 large eggs
3 large egg yolks
2 teaspoons vanilla extract
1 tablespoon fruit liquor such as Grand Marnier, Framboise, or
    Calvados
1 cup unsalted butter, at room temperature
¾ cup sugar
1 teaspoon kosher salt
1½ cups cake flour
2 to 4 tablespoons confectioners' sugar

Preheat the oven to 350 degrees. Lightly grease and flour a 9-inch springform pan. Line the bottom and sides with wax paper.

Place the white chocolate in a small saucepan and place it over a medium-sized saucepan of boiling water and cook over medium-high heat until it has melted. Set aside to cool.

Place the eggs, egg yolks, vanilla, and liquor in a small bowl and stir to combine.

Place the butter and sugar in the bowl of a mixer fitted with a paddle attachment, and mix until creamy and almost white, about 8 to 10 minutes.

While the butter is creaming, sift the salt and flour together. Add the flour, 2 tablespoons at a time, to the butter mixture, alternating with the egg mixture. Fold in the cooled white chocolate and transfer the mixture to the prepared pan.

Transfer to the middle rack of the oven and cook until golden and a toothpick inserted comes out clean, about 45 to 60 minutes Do not overcook. Remove the sides of the pan and cool for 10 minutes. Remove the bottom and then turn out on a platter.

Dust with confectioners' sugar.

Serve immediately, or cover and refrigerate up to 1 week, or double wrap in plastic and freeze up to 2 months.

Raelene's Flourless Chocolate Espresso Cake

For a clean, smooth edge, cut this cake with a knife that has been heated under hot running water and then dried.

SERVES 6

½ pound unsalted butter
4 ounces freshly brewed espresso coffee
⅔ cup light brown sugar
6 ounces semisweet chocolate, coarsely chopped
2 ounces unsweetened chocolate, coarsely chopped
4 large eggs, at room temperature
½ pint fresh raspberries, for garnish

Preheat the oven to 350 degrees. Butter and line the bottom of 1 loaf or 9-inch round pan with parchment paper.

Place the butter, espresso, and sugar in a medium saucepan over medium heat and bring to a very low boil. Stir until the sugar is dissolved. Add the chocolates and whisk until smooth. Set aside to cool.

Separate 2 of the eggs. Place 2 whole eggs and 2 egg yolks in a bowl and whisk together. Whisk the egg yolk mixture into the cooled chocolate.

Place 2 egg whites in a small mixing bowl and whisk until medium peaks form. Place about one-third of the egg whites in the chocolate mixture and gently mix. Fold in the remaining whites, making sure there are no large lumps.

Pour the batter into the prepared pan and place in a 9 x 13-inch pan. Pour enough cold water in the pan so that it comes up halfway. Smooth out the tops.

Transfer to the oven and bake until the top starts to crack and the center is no longer liquid, about 30 to 40 minutes. Remove the pan from the water bath and let cool. Cover and refrigerate overnight.

Cut around the sides to loosen the cake. Lift the cake off the pan and peel off the parchment. Cut into 6 slices and serve at room temperature, garnished with the raspberries.

Ginger Peach Crumble

*T*here's almost no better combination than ginger and peaches, especially when peaches are ripe and juicy. For me, the true test of a perfect peach is that you have to eat it over the sink.

Serve with whipped cream or vanilla bean or ginger ice cream.

If you can't find crystallized ginger, substitute 2 teaspoons finely grated fresh gingerroot.

SERVES 6 TO 8

6 large fresh peaches, cored and cut into large dice
Juice of one lemon
1 tablespoon plus 1 teaspoon finely crystallized ginger
1 tablespoon vanilla extract or brandy
2 tablespoons sugar
¼ teaspoon freshly grated nutmeg

For the topping:

1 cup all-purpose flour
1 cup rolled oats
½ cup coarsely chopped walnuts or pecans (optional)
½ cup sugar
¼ teaspoon freshly grated nutmeg
1 teaspoon ground ginger
1 teaspoon kosher salt
½ cup unsalted butter, cold and cut into small pieces

Preheat the oven to 375 degrees. Lightly butter an 8 x 8 baking pan.

To prepare the peaches: Place the peaches, lemon juice, ginger, vanilla or brandy, sugar, and nutmeg in the prepared pan and toss to combine.

To make the topping: Place the flour, oats, nuts, if desired, sugar, nutmeg, ginger, and salt in a medium bowl and toss to combine. Using a pastry cutter or two knives, add the butter and mix until crumbly. Sprinkle over the peaches and smooth out the top.

Transfer to the oven and bake until golden brown, about 25 minutes. Serve immediately or at room temperature.

Variations:

Pear Ginger Crumble: Substitute pears for the peaches and omit the vanilla extract.

Fig Raspberry Crumble: Substitute 15 black mission or calmyrna figs for the peaches and add 1 pint raspberries. Omit the vanilla, ginger, and nutmeg.

Chocolate Pie with Graham Cracker Crust

*I*nspired by eating lots of chocolate-covered graham crackers when I was growing up, this is the first chocolate dessert we had at Olives. I've been known to still sneak a few crackers from my kids.

MAKES ONE 8-INCH PIE

For the crust:

1 large egg
1 large egg yolk
⅓ cup sugar
¼ cup brown sugar
½ cup finely chopped semisweet chocolate
1½ cups finely ground graham crackers

For the filling:

½ pound semisweet chocolate, chopped
4 tablespoons unsalted butter, cut into small pieces
5 large egg yolks
1 large egg
⅓ cup sugar
Whipped cream, for garnish

Preheat the oven to 300 degrees.

To make the graham cracker crust: Place the egg and egg yolk in a small bowl and gradually whisk in the sugars. Add the chocolate and graham cracker crumbs and combine until moistened. Press into an 8-inch round pan until firm.

To make the chocolate filling: Place the chocolate and butter in a small pan over very low heat and cook until melted. Set aside to cool.

Place the egg yolks, egg, and sugar in a mixer and whip at high speed for 5 minutes or place in a bowl and mix with a hand mixer for 10 minutes. Set aside to cool.

Fold the cooled chocolate into the egg mixture and pour into the prepared pan. Transfer to the oven and bake until set, about 15 to 20 minutes. Set aside to cool to room temperature.

Serve immediately, garnished with whipped cream, or cover and refrigerate up to 24 hours.

Tiramisu

*T*iramisu, like crème brûlée, has become overdone and almost as popular (if not more popular) than cheesecake and apple pie. I'm afraid that my kids are going to expect tiramisu to be available at the ballpark! Although if it's well made, it might not be such a bad thing.

All kidding aside, tiramisu is a serious dessert and should be taken seriously. In my most humble opinion, I think this recipe makes the best tiramisu I've ever tasted which is why I can't take it off the Figs menu and why I include it here.

This is the most complicated dessert we make at Figs. Although this recipe looks arduous, most of it can be made ahead of time and assembled the day you want to serve it.

SERVES 8 TO 10

For the Tiramisu Cream:

This can be made up to three days ahead and refrigerated.

2 cups milk
½ vanilla bean, halved lengthwise and scraped
4 large egg yolks, at room temperature
1 large egg, at room temperature
1 cup sugar
½ cup plus 1 tablespoon cornstarch
¾ cup cream cheese (6 ounces), at room temperature
¼ cup mascarpone cheese (2 ounces), at room temperature
1 tablespoon unsalted butter, at room temperature

(continues)

1 cup heavy cream
1½ teaspoons vanilla extract
2 tablespoons confectioners' sugar

Place the milk and vanilla bean in a large saucepan over medium-high heat and scald the milk. Almost bring it to a boil, and when tiny bubbles begin to form (this should take about 5 minutes), remove the milk from the heat and let it steep for 30 minutes. Strain the milk and discard the bean. (Or you can do as we do at Figs: Dry the bean out and add it to white sugar to make vanilla sugar.)

While the milk is scalding, place the egg yolks and egg in a medium-sized bowl, mix to combine, and gradually whisk in the sugar. (If you do not do this gradually, the sugar will "cook" the egg yolks due to a chemical reaction.) Gradually whisk in the cornstarch.

Place the cream cheese, mascarpone cheese, and butter in a bowl and cream together until just smooth.

Drizzle half the milk mixture into the egg mixture, whisking all the while; then add this mixture back into the remaining milk mixture in the saucepan, whisking all the while. Place the saucepan over medium heat, whisking constantly, and cook until the cornstarch "blooms": When it bubbles once, count to five and then turn off the heat. The mixture will thicken very fast: Continue whisking until it has the consistency of mayonnaise. As soon as it does, strain it into the bowl of the mixer with the cream cheese, pushing the mixture through the strainer with a spatula and eliminating any bits of cooked egg that might appear. On low speed, combine the egg and cream cheese until the color is consistent.

Transfer to a shallow pan and place a layer of plastic wrap directly on top of the mixture, stopping any skin from forming. Place in the refrigerator.

Just prior to assembling the tiramisu: Place the cream, vanilla, and confectioners' sugar in a mixer and whip until it forms stiff peaks. Gently fold half the whipped cream into the mascarpone cream with a rubber spatula. Repeat with the remaining whipped cream.

For the Coffee Simple Syrup:

5 tablespoons sugar
½ cup water
1½ cups double-strength coffee, or espresso

Place the sugar and water in a small saucepan and bring to a boil, stirring until the sugar is completely dissolved. Add the coffee or espresso and stir until combined. Set aside to cool.

For the Genoise:

This simple genoise is an untraditional recipe; it is made in one bowl and should be made one day ahead. You will probably have leftover genoise but better safe than sorry; use it as a tasty way to clean out the whipped cream bowl. It can also be used to make a trifle.

1¼ cups all-purpose flour, plus additional for dusting the pan
½ cup cornstarch
8 large eggs
1 cup sugar
2 teaspoons vanilla extract
¾ teaspoon almond extract
1½ tablespoons unsalted butter, melted

Preheat the oven to 350 degrees. Spray a cookie sheet with 1-inch sides or a jelly-roll pan with vegetable spray and line it with parchment or wax paper. Spray the paper and sprinkle it with flour.

Sift the flour and cornstarch together into a bowl. Set aside.

Place the eggs and sugar in the metal bowl of a mixer and whisk together. Place a medium saucepan over high heat and fill halfway with water. When the

water is hot, place the metal bowl in it and cook until the sugar dissolves, whisking all the while. Do not allow the bottom of the metal bowl to touch the bottom of the saucepan. Return the bowl to the mixer and whisk at high speed until cooled, about 5 to 6 minutes.

Turn the speed to low and while the mixer is running, add the vanilla and almond extracts and then gradually add the flour mixture. As soon as the flour is incorporated, add the melted butter. Turn off the mixer as soon as the butter is incorporated. Stir once with a rubber spatula and then pour onto the prepared sheet or pan. Have the bowl as close to the pan as possible so that you move the batter as little as possible and don't move the air around a lot. Spread the mixture evenly and gently transfer to the oven. Bake until it is golden brown, starts to pull away from the sides, and springs back when touched gently, about 14 to 16 minutes.

To Assemble:

Cocoa powder, for garnish

Avoid using the stove or dishwasher while assembling the tiramisu; the kitchen should be as cool as possible.

All the ingredients should be completely cooled.

Now, for the hard part: Cut the genoise into 4 even rectangles. Place each block, 1 at a time, on a cutting board and slice it horizontally with a serrated knife, into 2 to 3 thin slices. Place 1 layer of genoise in the bottom of a 10-inch round springform pan or a 2-quart bowl. Drizzle about ⅔ to ¾ cup coffee simple syrup over the cake, allowing it to soak in. Place half the tiramisu cream on the genoise and dust evenly with cocoa powder. Cover with the remaining genoise and repeat the process again, dusting the top of the tiramisu heavily with the cocoa powder.

Cover with plastic wrap and refrigerate at least 4 hours or up to 2 days.

Raspberry Sauce

This is a basic fruit sauce that we use on a myriad of ice creams, Vanilla Pound Cake (page 209), and White-Chocolate Challah Pudding (page 206). You can substitute blueberries or strawberries for the raspberries, if you prefer.

MAKES 1 CUP

4 cups fresh or frozen raspberries, thawed
2 teaspoons fresh lemon juice
6 tablespoons sugar
Water

Place the raspberries, lemon juice, and sugar in a blender and process until puréed. Transfer to a strainer and push the solids through. This may take several batches. Discard the seeds and membranes.

Add water if it is too thick. Use immediately, or cover and refrigerate up to 1 week.

Caramel Sauce

*R*ich, sweet, and smooth, this sauce is delicious on White-Chocolate Challah Pudding (page 206) or Vanilla Pound Cake (page 209) or drizzled on vanilla ice cream.

MAKES 1¼ CUPS

½ cup sugar
½ teaspoon kosher salt
1 tablespoon water
½ teaspoon lemon juice
1 cup heavy cream
1½ teaspoons unsalted butter
1 teaspoon vanilla extract or bourbon

Place the sugar, salt, water, and lemon juice in a small saucepan over medium-high heat and bring to a boil. Swirl the pan but do not stir the sugar. Cook until the sugar is dark brown but not smoking. Remove from the heat and let cool slightly, about 3 minutes.

Add the cream in a steady stream, whisking all the while, and when the cream is fully incorporated, place the pan over medium-low heat and bring back to a boil. Simmer until thick bubbles form and the mixture has reduced by almost half. Remove from the heat and cool for 10 minutes. Add the butter, a little at a time, and the vanilla or bourbon. (If you want, you can refrigerate this up to 2 weeks and reheat at low before proceeding.)

If sugar crystals have formed on the sides of the pan, brush them down with cold water and a nonplastic bristled pastry brush.

Use immediately, or cover and refrigerate up to 1 week.

Variation:

Mango Caramel Sauce: Add 2 mangoes, 1 puréed and 1 diced.

Mail Order Sources

Cheddar Cheese Powder:

Cabot Creamery
1-800-453-8927

Truffle Oil and Spices:

Dean and Deluca
New York City
1-800-221-7714

Spices:

Penzey's
Wisconsin
414-574-0277

INDEX

METRIC EQUIVALENCIES

Liquid and Dry Measure Equivalencies

Customary	Metric
¼ teaspoon	1.25 milliliters
½ teaspoon	2.5 milliliters
1 teaspoon	5 milliliters
1 tablespoon	15 milliliters
1 fluid ounce	30 milliliters
¼ cup	60 milliliters
⅓ cup	80 milliliters
½ cup	120 milliliters
1 cup	240 milliliters
1 pint (*2 cups*)	480 milliliters
1 quart (*4 cups, 32 ounces*)	960 milliliters (*.96 liter*)
1 gallon (*4 quarts*)	3.84 liters
1 ounce (*by weight*)	28 grams
¼ pound (*4 ounces*)	114 grams
1 pound (*16 ounces*)	454 grams
2.2 pounds	1 kilogram (*1000 grams*)

Oven Temperature Equivalencies

Description	°Fahrenheit	°Celsius
Cool	200	90
Very slow	250	120
Slow	300–325	150–160
Moderately slow	325–350	160–180
Moderate	350–375	180–190
Moderately hot	375–400	190–200
Hot	400–450	200–230
Very hot	450–500	230–260

Printed in the United States
By Bookmasters